The Shape of Change

No organisations, change initiative, or stakeholder is ever the same. The way business change management is shaped to work with and get the best out of every different change situation makes a vital contribution to the success of the change.

The Shape of Change is the first business change management book to focus solely on the practical challenges of how to plan, implement, and embed successful business change initiatives in a wide range of organisations from the business change manager's point of view. It focusses on shaping every different change approach to take into consideration each individual situation, including organisational culture, the type and impact of the change initiative, the attitudes and concerns of stakeholders, and the potential for resistance within the organisation. Using a series of example change initiatives in private, public, and non-profit sectors, it describes the change management journey, highlighting key points where business change management interventions are essential, and exploring how it feels to undertake business change initiatives in a wide range of situations, from communicating the initial change idea to ensuring the change is embedded and working well in business as usual.

Accessible and comprehensive, *The Shape of Change* is relevant to anyone working in or planning organisational change.

Nicola Busby is an experienced business change manager specialising in cultural and behavioural change in the public, private, and non-profit sectors. Her recent clients include Penguin Random House, The Financial Ombudsman Service, The Houses of Parliament, and the National Childbirth Trust. She is the author of Chapter 7, 'Change Readiness, Planning and Measurement', in *The Effective Change Manager's Handbook*.

Nicola Busby captures the work and process of supporting a change initiative in a lively, practical and down-to earth way. She describes how different phases of change can be approached, giving clear examples and illustrations. I particularly liked the human reality checks embedded in her descriptions of "this is how it actually feels to help change happen". I expect that this book will prove a good friend to many business change managers.

Richard Smith, business change practitioner and lead author of *The Effective Change Manager's Handbook*

At last, a book that supports the change journey by providing step by step advice and guidance on how to deliver effective change from the early stages of inception through to embedding into an organisation and beyond. This book will help many organisations to not only recognise the importance of managing change but how to do this in a way that will promote successful and sustainable change.

Joanne McCormick, Head of Operational Change, Penguin Random House

The Shape of Change

A Guide to Planning, Implementing and Embedding Organisational Change

Nicola Busby

Routledge
Taylor & Francis Group

LONDON AND NEW YORK

First published 2017
by Routledge
2 Park Square, Milton Park, Abingdon, Oxon OX14 4RN

and by Routledge
711 Third Avenue, New York, NY 10017

Routledge is an imprint of the Taylor & Francis Group, an informa business

© 2017 Nicola Busby

British Library Cataloguing-in-Publication Data
A catalogue record for this book is available from the British Library

Library of Congress Cataloging-in-Publication Data
Names: Busby, Nicola, 1974– author.
Title: The shape of change : a guide to planning, implementing and embedding organisational change / Nicola Busby.
Description: Abingdon, Oxon ; New York, NY : Routledge, 2017. | Includes bibliographical references and index.
Identifiers: LCCN 2017003319 (print) | LCCN 2017020210 (ebook) | ISBN 9781315455457 (eBook) | ISBN 9781138210332 (hardback) | ISBN 9781138210349 (pbk.)
Subjects: LCSH: Organizational change.
Classification: LCC HD58.8 (ebook) | LCC HD58.8 .B8848 2017 (print) | DDC 658.4/06—dc23
LC record available at https://lccn.loc.gov/2017003319

ISBN: 9781138210332 (hbk)
ISBN: 9781138210349 (pbk)
ISBN: 9781315455457 (ebk)

Typeset in Bembo
by Apex CoVantage, LLC

To Derek, Kathy, and Tony. With all my love and thanks.

Contents

Figures

Introduction

The business of change

Whenever I run training sessions on business change, I begin by asking delegates to think about when they have experienced change – either in a work environment or elsewhere – and to answer the following questions:

1   When change has gone well, what happened to make it go well?
2   When change has gone badly, what happened to make it go badly?
3   How did you feel during the change?

Figure 0.1 shows the comments which invariably arise.

These answers encapsulate what business change management is all about. It focusses on the opinions, emotions, and actions of everyone involved in the change, with the aim of increasing positivity and engagement.

Every individual required to plan, make decisions, and implement the change should be able to support the change and contribute effectively. Every user affected by the change needs to make the decision to participate in the change and make the effort to do things differently. It is only when these two things happen that the benefits of the change can be realised and success is achieved. Successful change not only means a better organisation through the realisation of specific benefits but can also lead to an overall improvement in morale, motivation, and confidence – and this can only be a good thing for both employers and employees.

There are three basic parts to initiating change within an organisation:

The object of the change could be anything within the organisation, for example a new piece of software or a new target operating model, a focus on a new customer base or a shift in culture and core values. The object may not always be tangible but should always be possible to describe, even when the change is in very early discussion stages or involves an emergent approach.

The associated activities represent the ways in which people will do things differently after the object of the change is implemented, for example processes to accompany new software or reporting lines into new managers, building relationships with new customers or basing decision making on an amended set of values. New activities can generally be identified, and people will need to learn how to carry them out and transition from current activities to new ones.

When change has gone well	When change has gone badly
• Clearly understood the need for change • Strong sponsorship and leadership of change • Change was properly planned and managed • Clear, two-way communication • Widespread staff involvement • Key people empowered • Identified benefits of change – what's in it for me *Felt empowered, excited, motivated, proud, energised, optimistic*	• Didn't understand the reason for the change – change for change's sake • Lack of understanding of impact • No sponsorship or visible leadership • Ineffective communications – one way with no chance to feedback • Change imposed and happened too quickly • Lack of trust • Lack of support for staff *Felt scared, powerless, unsettled, demotivated, lost, frustrated*

Figure 0.1 Common experiences of business change

The people involved and affected by the change – how they feel about the change and therefore how they choose to act in relation to it. Will they support or resist it? Are they willing and able to be involved in planning and designing the change? Will they embed new ways of working to realise the benefits?

Figure 0.2 illustrates the scope of business change management, with the shaded area illustrating the business change manager's responsibility to take the lead on all issues relating to the people involved in and affected by the change, including where their input is required to plan, develop, and implement the object of the change and the associated activities.

Business change management encompasses a wide range of activities, including (but not restricted to):

- Increasing buy-in for the change, communicating a compelling picture of the future, overcoming resistance, addressing people's concerns;
- Ensuring that the changes are suitable, workable, and acceptable for all affected users;
- Ensuring the change is owned and supported throughout the organisation;
- Enabling change leaders to take people issues into consideration when making decisions about the change;
- Ensuring all affected users know why the change is happening, what they are being asked to do differently, and how they are going to be supported in learning and trying out new things;
- Ensuring new ways of working are sustainable and embedded after implementation so the benefits can be realised.

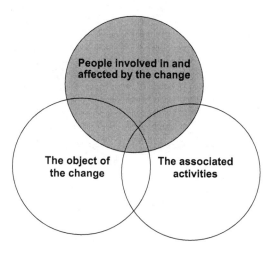

Figure 0.2 The scope of the business change manager

Every change is different

It is vital for business change managers to understand there is no 'one size fits all' approach to change management. No two organisations, stakeholders, or change initiatives are ever the same, and every situation will require different interventions at different times to make the change successful.

Consequently, we need to shape our business change approach for every different change initiative we tackle. This does not mean a completely new set of interventions each time, but it does mean that a number of factors need to be taken into consideration for each initiative and these will determine how we approach the change. Factors include the culture of the organisation, the attitudes and concerns of the stakeholders involved, the scale and impact of the change initiative, and the amount and type of resistance expected. The change approach will also need to be revised and refined constantly throughout the change journey. A linear set of activities, planned in detail at the beginning of the change and executed at pre-determined times in a pre-agreed way, will not result in successful change. The shape of our approach is constantly changing, developing, and morphing in new ways depending on the reactions we get to our interventions and the information we receive as we build relationships with our stakeholders.

If you want to understand how to shape your approach to change according to your specific circumstances, this book is for you. It will guide you through a typical change journey exploring the points where business change interventions are most needed, explain how to obtain the information you need to shape your change approach, and investigate how to undertake your change interventions to ensure your business changes are as successful as possible, time after time.

The role of the business change manager

Throughout the book, the term 'business change manager' is used to describe anyone who is responsible for the people aspects of a change initiative. The role may be known by a number of other titles, for example business change analyst, change and communications manager, business change lead, business lead, engagement lead, business readiness lead, or business transition manager.

As well as the wide variety of titles, there are various roles and positions for business change managers. Like so much else about business change, the best way to position the role depends on the culture, history, and environment of the individual organisation and the type of change being undertaken. Many change initiatives are run through structured projects and programmes, but others are executed as part of business as usual activities or continual improvement initiatives. Here are a few examples of the more common positions you may find yourself working in as a business change manager:

The business change manager in a project

The business change manager is responsible for all the people aspects of a change project and is the link between the project and the affected areas of the organisation. In many organisations, projects are set up and run using standard project methodologies (e.g. PRINCE2, APM, Agile) or a bespoke in-house methodology, and key roles such as project manager, project sponsor, and project board are used.

The business change manager reports to the project manager and needs to work closely with them and other key roles within the project to make sure everyone is clear on their individual areas of responsibility. For example the project manager may be responsible for setting the dates for the change to be implemented, but the business change manager is responsible for agreeing these dates with stakeholders and ensuring all users are fully prepared beforehand.

The business change manager looks at all project options and decisions from the viewpoint of the stakeholders and tends to work through the project manager to influence project decision makers. For example the business change manager may work with stakeholders to examine whether proposed implementation dates will adversely impact business as usual activities and feed this back to the project manager. The project manager will then incorporate this information into their roll out proposals to take to the project board for final decision.

If there is more than one change project happening within the organisation, the business change managers need to work together to coordinate the impact on stakeholders. Depending on the size of the changes, the business change manager may work on more than one project at a time.

What does this look like in real life?

Figure 0.3 shows the organisational structure for the office move at Spark Clearholme, where the business change manager sat within the project.

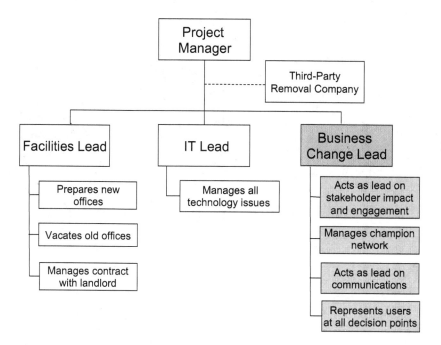

Figure 0.3 The business change manager in a project

Known as the business change lead, this role was responsible for all the people-focussed activities during the office move. The business change lead worked closely with the project manager and facilities and technology leads to coordinate change activities which needed input from other parts of the project, such as the following:

- Arranging tours of the new building in conjunction with the facilities lead. The facilities lead arranged the tour itinerary and access to the building, and the business change lead advertised and booked users onto the tours, managing any questions and feedback.
- Organising Move Action Packs in conjunction with the project manager. The project manager worked with the third-party removal company and the facilities and technology leads to agree the logistics of the move and what users needed to do to prepare. The business change lead then incorporated this information into Move Action Packs and supported users as they undertook all necessary preparations for the move, feeding back any related questions and suggestions to the project manager.

The business change lead was also responsible for identifying and managing people-focussed risks and feeding any people issues up to the project manager, who would escalate to the project sponsor and board where necessary. The business change lead ensured all business change activities were included in the project plan and updated them frequently throughout the project as the change approach evolved in light of user information and actions.

This particular business change role was for two days a week, and the business change lead worked on other change projects in the organisation concurrently. It was rare for the role to take exactly two days, with more or less time needed each week depending on the stage of the project and the needs of stakeholders. This was difficult to plan in advance, so strong time management skills and the ability to juggle and prioritise change management tasks across a number of projects were needed. It was important that the business change manager worked in the organisation full time as, although the role itself was not full time, activities needed to be planned around stakeholder availability, and urgent user issues and queries could arise at any time. If the business change manager had been present in the organisation for only two days a week, someone else would have had to pick up this work for the remaining days, leading to inefficiencies within the project team and confusion for stakeholders.

The business change manager in a programme

Change initiatives run as programmes are generally larger and more complex than individual projects. They may consist of a number of separate projects or workstreams which deliver specific but interrelated changes. The culmination of all the projects is one strategic or large-scale change which is designed to bring clear benefits to the organisation.

All the tasks relating to project-related business change remain true for the business change manager in a programme, with the additional need to coordinate the people-related activities across all the interrelated projects and workstreams. This is to avoid the confusion, irritation, and inefficiencies experienced by both the users and the programme team if each project tries to engage users separately. The business change manager also needs to understand the business impact of each project clearly so they can help the programme team schedule activities to minimise disruption for individual users and the wider organisation and ensure appropriate support is in place to help users transition to new ways of working introduced by any project or workstream.

What does this look like in real life?

Figure 0.4 shows the organisational structure for the Electronic Document Records Management System (EDRMS) programme at Burntwood County Council, where the business change manager sat alongside the programme manager and managed the business change for the programme.

The EDRMS programme was a temporary team set up to deliver the EDRMS implementation and accompanying behavioural changes to Burntwood County Council. The business change manager role was a full-time, senior position within the programme. The business change manager managed a change team

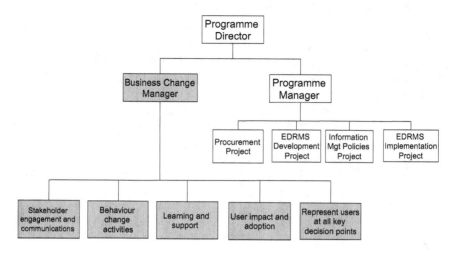

Figure 0.4 The business change manager in a programme

consisting of a communications officer, four user support officers (see Chapter 7 for more on these roles) and three trainers who between them engaged, communicated with, and supported all individuals affected by the change. The business change manager played an active part in the governance of the programme, attending all board meetings and liaising regularly with board members and other key senior stakeholders on decisions affecting users. The business change manager was also responsible for coaching and mentoring board members and other key stakeholders on various aspects of business change, including their responsibilities as leaders of the change, how to prepare for the likely impacts of implementation, and how to deal with the business change risks and issues throughout the programme.

The business change manager liaised closely with the project managers to coordinate all people-related aspects of the projects. For example the EDRMS Development Project worked with the business change manager to find users to test and pilot the system and the Information Management Policy project worked with the business change manager to set up and run a local information champion group across Burntwood. The business change manager also coordinated all communications from the programme and projects through a regular programme newsletter and ensured all training needs from the projects were combined so affected users did not have to attend multiple training sessions.

The business change manager was also responsible for maximising any programme benefits resulting from user adoption of the change. This was done by supporting relevant users to adopt and embed the changes needed to realise the benefits and making sure that the benefits were taken into consideration during any decision-making activities undertaken by the sponsor and programme board.

The business change manager as subject matter expert

The business change subject matter expert offers internal consultancy to change initiatives across an organisation. They may sit in a project management office if the organisation has one but can be positioned virtually anywhere within the organisation.

The subject matter expert has overall responsibility for the design and execution of the change management approach for all change initiatives and projects and for building the change capability within the organisation. They coach, train, and support project managers, operational managers, and change agents in the people aspects of change. They also coach and mentor senior decision makers in the organisation who are responsible for governing and leading change.

The subject matter expert develops a holistic view of the effect of change on the organisation and keeps track of where engagement and impacts from different change initiatives are being felt by the same stakeholders. They liaise with all others working in change to coordinate engagement and minimise cumulative impacts where possible. If formal project methodologies are used in the organisation, the subject matter expert ensures the business change approach fits with the project approach and develops any business change templates needed.

What does this look like in real life?

Figure 0.5 shows the organisational structure for the project management office at Spark Clearholme, showing the role of the business change subject matter expert.

This interesting and varied role required a strategic approach to change as it focused on developing Spark Clearholme's capability to manage change as well as leading on the people aspects of all the change currently happening in the organisation.

The subject matter expert worked with a wide range of stakeholders, coaching and mentoring leaders, and operational managers across the organisation. They devised a high level business change approach for the organisation and supported individual project and programme managers and business change leads to adapt it for their particular change initiatives. They also coordinated business change activities and impacts across different projects and programmes and connected people working on change initiatives with each other, and relevant stakeholders, from across the organisation.

The business change project manager

This is effectively a project manager role for change initiatives which have big organisational impacts and the need for substantial stakeholder engagement.

As well as managing all the business change activities needed for the change, the business change project manager is responsible for the delivery of the project, including managing the project board, producing all project documentation, developing and controlling the project plan, managing risks and issues, and coordinating all workstreams and project activities.

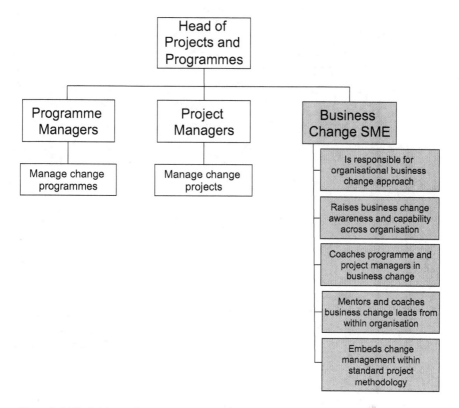

Figure 0.5 The business change manager as subject matter expert

What does this look like in real life?

Figure 0.6 shows the organisational structure for the e-file project at Mayer & Co Law Firm, which was run by a business change project manager.

This was a full-time role split between approximately 60% project and 40% business change activities. The business change project manager was the single point of contact for all senior stakeholders, including the project sponsor and board, so they could ensure a business focus for all project decisions. The business change project manager also ensured that all project activities focused on users, which increased support and buy-in for the change.

Despite adequate planning and organisation skills, the business change project manager often had to spend time dealing with urgent project issues, leaving reduced amounts of time for real business change work. For example there were continuing issues with the e-file technology which needed attention and used up time allocated to helping the organisation prepare for and implement the change.

The role of business change project manager was highly pressured and involved juggling lots of responsibilities. Skills and expertise in both project

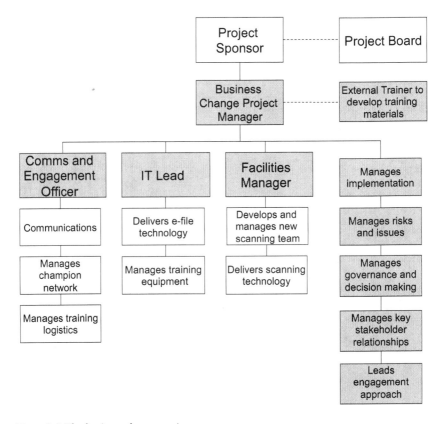

Figure 0.6 The business change project manager

management and business change management were needed, and there was often internal tension between which should take priority. For example does the 'project manager' recommend that the project sticks to original roll out dates even though the software contains bugs which will irritate users, or does the 'business change manager' recommend that the roll out is delayed until the bugs are fixed, increasing user acceptance and adoption but costing money and delaying the project? (See Chapter 6 for more discussion about the potential tensions between delivery and change.)

Managing a change initiative outside of a project environment

Not all change initiatives are run as formal projects or programmes. This may be because the initiative comes from within an operational department and is implemented as part of business as usual continual improvement or because the organisation does not have an established project or programme function.

Absence of a formal project environment does not mean that change cannot be implemented and embedded successfully. However, it is worth bearing in mind that, along with business change management, project and programme frameworks have evolved as a response to traditionally high failure rates for change initiatives. If you are planning a high risk or complex change, you may want to explore the possibility of using a formal project approach, even if this is new to your organisation. (If this is the case, remember that the introduction of a new project methodology is a business change initiative in itself and needs to be managed accordingly.)

If you are working in an organisation which has an established project or programme function, make sure you engage with it for your change initiative. It may be tempting to bypass official methodologies which seem time consuming, constraining, and complicated, but they will save you effort in the long run. Successfully implementing change is often far more complicated than it first looks, and the project function should have access to all the right decision makers, resources, and expertise needed to overcome barriers and deal with problems.

If you find yourself working on a change initiative that is not being managed as a formal project, there are a few conditions which still need to be in place to increase the chance of success, including:

- A compelling reason for the change, including convincing drivers for change and a shared understanding of what is going to change and what the benefits will be;
- A single point of accountability, ideally an effective and respected leader, who is responsible for overseeing the change and making all the key decisions;
- A clear understanding of which teams and individuals across the organisation will be needed to implement the change and agreement from them that they will cooperate.

What does this look like in real life?

Figure 0.7 shows the organisational structure for the restructure at Workout!, which was managed outside of a project environment.

The business change manager was responsible for all aspects of the change, similar to a business change project manager role but without the formal project disciplines. Workout! did not have a formal project or programme management approach, as most changes up until that point had been smaller scale, emergent, and dealt with as continual improvement. However, this large-scale, transformative change initiative was still successful for the following reasons:

- **A compelling reason to change:** The transformation was needed to meet new government legislation and ensure the survival of the organisation. It had been planned in detail by the CEO, her executive team, and the board of directors. Therefore, there was a shared understanding of what the change involved and what the future would look like, right to the top of the organisation.

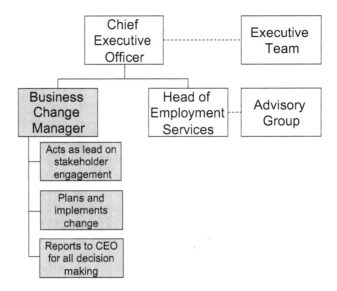

Figure 0.7 Business change manager outside of a project environment

- **A single point of accountability:** The CEO was responsible for overseeing the change and making all key decisions. Charismatic and well respected, there was minimal resistance and objections amongst her senior management colleagues in relation to how the change was led.
- **Cooperation from all who needed to be involved:** As this was a key change initiative for the organisation led by the CEO, all the teams involved, including technology, HR, finance, and operations, willingly gave all the support needed to implement the change.

What do you need to know to work in business change?

Successful business change managers have an understanding of the main change management theories and activities and know to shape them to make the best out of different situations. They also have high levels of emotional intelligence and well-developed people skills such as facilitation, negotiation, influencing, and active listening.

In addition, there are three attributes which are fundamental for anyone working in business change.

The ability to see the world through the filters of other people

Just as light through a lens refracts into many different coloured shards, all actions or decisions in relation to a change initiative distort through the filters of individuals into a range of different interpretations, emotions, and subsequent reactions. These distortions contribute significantly to the challenges of working with people through business change.

Everyone working on your change initiative will have a different focus. For example your project manager will concentrate on plans, dependencies, and risks, and your change leader will be interested in finances, benefits, and strategic fit. It is your job as business change manager to check every decision and action relating to the change through the filter of your stakeholders, ask 'what might people feel about this?', and manage all potential interpretations, distortions, and reactions. If you cannot empathise, imagine, and easily view the world through the eyes of other people, you will struggle to do this effectively.

The ability to deal with uncertainty

Implementing a change means introducing something that has never been done before in the organisation. This means there is no set way of approaching it, no knowledge about the best way to implement it, and no evidence that it will work. This is very unsettling and can sometimes feel like the solid earth has moved to shifting sand beneath your feet. As a business change manager, you need to be able to not only deal with the uncertainty yourself but also support others through it.

Not everything you try will be successful, so you need to be comfortable with taking risks, be willing to try new things, and have the energy and stamina to deal with frequent issues and complaints. If things do go wrong, as they inevitably will in such unchartered territory, you need enough self-confidence and belief to be able to pick yourself up, dust yourself off, learn relevant lessons, and move on.

The tendency to be inquisitive

When working with people, things are rarely what they first appear to be. You constantly need to ask yourself 'why is this happening?' and avoid making assumptions about how people will react or take what people say at face value. You need to continually observe and analyse situations, personalities, cultures, reactions, and behaviours, looking for the true messages and meaning which hide deeply beneath surface emotions and actions and may lead to the success or failure of the change. You can never be complacent and assume that just because an activity or approach worked last time it will work again – every situation and stakeholder is unique, and you need to remain alert and reactive to all information and signals at all times.

How does it feel to work in business change?

Business change is neither straightforward nor easy and can sometimes be downright tough. However, it is endlessly challenging and fascinating, and there is always something new to learn. Carried out with care, business change management can be the one thing that makes the difference between success and failure of a change initiative and can make an enormous difference to the welfare of the people involved. It is often only when you see the difference that your business change interventions make to people's well-being that you realise that the effort is worthwhile. (Some advice on measuring and monitoring your change interventions can be found in Chapter 6.) If you manage business change well, it can turn out to be an extremely rewarding and satisfying role.

References and further reading

Cameron, E. and Green, M. 2009. *Making Sense of Change Management.* 2nd ed. London: Kogan Page

Goleman, D. 1996. *Emotional Intelligence: Why It Can Matter More Than IQ.* London: Bloomsbury

Rees, W. David and Porter, C. 2001. *Skills of Management.* 5th ed. London: Thomson Learning

Smith, R., King, D., Sidhu, R. and Skelsey, D. 2013. *The Effective Change Manager: The Change Management Body of Knowledge.* Sydney: The Change Management Institute

Smith, R., King, D., Sidhu, R. and Skelsey, D., eds. 2014. *The Effective Change Manager's Handbook.* London: Kogan Page

1 Shaping the need for change

Introducing change into organisations is disruptive, costly, and risky. In order for change to be successful, there needs to be very strong reasons why it needs to happen. These reasons are called the drivers for change.

Drivers for change tend to fall into three main categories:

To improve the organisation: this can be done in a number of ways, including:

- Changing the organisation internally to become more efficient or effective;
- Altering the goods or services produced or branching out into different customer segments to take advantage of opportunities in the market;
- Improving the reputation of the organisation to fulfil moral obligations, motivate staff, and attract customers.

To adapt to an external event: this can be in response to anything that happens in the world outside of the organisation, including:

- The advent of new laws, regulations, or policies that affect the organisation;
- Changes in the economy or society which affect the behaviour of customers;
- Increased competition from other organisations.

Advances in technology: technology has a place in most change, but some change initiatives exist purely because of technological advances, for example:

- Upgrading technological infrastructure or software;
- Implementing enterprise software to perform business functions such as order processing, accounting, and customer relationship management;
- Dealing with outdated goods and services or organisational capabilities due to advances in technology.

Organisational changes of any significant size usually have more than one driver. Often the case for change becomes compelling enough only when a number of drivers combine to make undertaking change less risky than the consequences of keeping things as they are.

Table 1.1 gives some examples of change initiatives, showing the main drivers for the change:

Table 1.1 The drivers for example change initiatives

Change Initiative	Drivers
Burntwood EDRMS Introducing better information management across the county council	A recent government directive requires all UK county councils to review their information management practices
	A recent data protection breach damaged the reputation of Burntwood and put users at risk
	Information management could be more efficient and the quality of documents produced could be improved
Mayer & Co E-file Moving the law firm from paper to electronic caseloads	Potential customers not accessing the law firm due to outdated communication methods
	There is a high risk of losing important and confidential paper files in transit
	The firm is shortly moving to new offices with less storage space, so there will be limited room for paper files
Workout! Restructure Standardising and professionalising the services offered to customers	New legislation has recently been introduced stating that all UK charities must show public benefit
	A recognition that the quality of service given to customers needs to be improved
	A need to have greater control and visibility of services and finances in order to grow the organisation
Spark Clearholme Office Move Relocating the newly merged organisation from four buildings into one	Leases of current buildings are shortly coming to an end with no chance of renewal
	Increased opportunities for more collaborative working and time saved if all teams are located in one building
	The move will consolidate the merger and encourage the staff to think of themselves as belonging to one organisation
Spark Clearholme Marketing Campaign Planner Standardising the software used by marketing teams to plan campaigns	Information about marketing campaigns are currently recorded in lots of different ways
	Management data are needed to learn about best practice from marketing campaigns
	Marketing practices need to improve to keep ahead of the competition in an increasingly crowded marketplace

The business change manager may be involved with identifying drivers and advocating change, but this is more normally done by business leaders and strategy professionals or operational teams. It is usually only after the decision to change has been taken that active business change management starts, and the first activities needed include:

- Putting foundations in place for successful change
- Creating a compelling vision for the change
- Communicating early messages about the change.

Putting the foundations in place for successful change

Ideas for change can come from anywhere within the organisation, including:

- From the top down, when change ideas are generated by senior leaders as part of the organisation's strategy;
- From the ground up, when staff within operational areas generate ideas to solve local issues or exploit local opportunities.

Change ideas generated from the top down

Change ideas generated from senior leaders as part of the organisation's strategy tend to be larger and more complex than those coming from within operational areas. Senior leaders focus on the organisation as a whole, rather than specialising in separate operational areas, and so can initiate changes which affect multiple departments and teams. They also have more power and influence than those sitting within operational areas, greater access to resources, and the ability to prioritise what the organisation focusses on. This means that changes generated from the top should have many of the factors which will contribute to success already in place, including strong leadership support, good strategic fit, compelling drivers for change, and enough resources and management attention to execute the change properly.

Often, the main challenge with making top down change successful is ensuring that the proposed changes can realistically be implemented in the affected parts of the organisation. Senior leaders can be quite removed from the day to day workings of the organisation and may think that a change initiative will be easier to implement than it really is, generally through underestimating the effect on cultures and behaviours.

Therefore, a major role of business change in the early days of a top down change is to encourage the senior leaders who generated the idea to consult with the areas of the organisation which are going to be affected by the change. Representatives from these areas can add real value at this stage by offering insights into how people, systems and cultures work on the ground, and therefore how much they will be affected by the change initiative. They can also advise on how easily or otherwise they feel changes would be accepted and could quite possibly come up with alternative ideas which could still achieve the desired goal but make the future far more palatable for their colleagues, increasing the chances of success.

Make sure you choose your organisational representatives carefully. They need to be trusted by both their colleagues and senior leaders and they need to be able to assess the ideas as impartially as possible. They should be sympathetic to the need for change and work together with the decision makers for the very best outcome for the organisation as a whole, and not just their affected areas or individual teams.

Box 1.1   Business representation in the early days of Burntwood EDRMS

Spurred on by a number of compelling drivers for change, the CEO included an update of information management practices in Burntwood County Council's new three-year strategy. A small project team was set up to investigate options, and a panel of evaluators was created. The panel consisted of all the senior leaders with an interest in the initiative but also included two representatives from within the operational areas of the organisation. These representatives were chosen because they were well respected by their colleagues and had a good understanding of how the organisation worked. They were able to give an indication of how much impact each option would have on different operational areas in terms of working practices, behaviours, and cultures, and they played a significant role in shaping the eventual solution.

Change ideas generated from the ground up

Change ideas generated by operational areas to solve local issues or exploit local opportunities are generally smaller in scope and impact fewer areas of the organisation than strategic changes generated by senior leaders. At least, that is how they may seem initially.

One of the key activities needed at the early stages of these ideas is to assess whether the changes impact only the local area, and therefore can be implemented locally as part of business as usual, or whether they are actually bigger than they seem and need to be managed as larger organisational changes. Two indicators may help with this assessment:

If more than one area within the organisation is working separately to solve the same problems or try out the same ideas. This may indicate that the scope of change is larger than originally thought, the impact on the organisation may be greater than currently expected, and there may be opportunities for increasing the benefits of the change by approaching the problem more holistically. If so, the change becomes strategic and will need senior leadership, resources, and engagement from across the organisation to be successful. Therefore, it should be treated as a larger organisational change.

If the change impacts more than just the local area who had the idea. Implementing local change initiatives often involve more functions and departments than originally expected. It is important to ascertain who needs to be involved in and may be affected by any local change initiative before the change commences; otherwise, you may be in for a nasty shock later on. Many change initiatives have been undermined because those involved have consciously or unconsciously overlooked the impact and consequences beyond the immediate team. The stakeholder identification exercise outlined in Chapter 4 will help you understand who needs to be involved in and is affected by your change.

If the change does involve more than the initial local area, then managing it as a bigger organisational change will greatly increase its chance of success. There is sometimes reluctance from local areas to relinquish control of their change idea and watch it take on a new and different life of its own, but ultimately time, money, and emotional anguish will be saved if the change is a large-scale success rather than a smaller-scale failure.

Box 1.2   When a local initiative is actually a major organisational change

The marketing team at Spark Clearholme decided they wanted learn more about the many marketing campaigns the organisation ran for its products each year. Therefore, without consulting any other departments within the organisation, they purchased a piece of software from an external company in which to enter the marketing and financial information for every marketing campaign, with a view to being able to compare activities and costs of each campaign and learn more about what works best.

Once the software was bought, the team soon realised that in order for it to be successfully implemented and used, there would need to be involvement from many other departments in the organisation. The technology department needed to install the software, link it up with other Spark Clearholme technology to automatically feed in certain marketing information, and ensure that it was secure and compatible with the rest of the technology in the organisation. The finance department needed to undergo a major change to their working practices to ensure that all financial information relating to marketing campaigns was entered into the software, and the business intelligence team needed to create meaningful management reports so the required lessons could be learned. In order to train the marketing assistants and finance officers to use the software, Learning and Development needed to grant access to rooms and trainers, and HR needed to create and recruit a new role within the marketing team to support everyone in using the software once implemented.

All of these activities involved far more complexity and impacted significantly more people than the marketing department ever imagined. After all, the software was only a simple solution designed to meet a specific need. The team was unable to implement the change on their own and, after months of failed attempts, the project had to be incorporated into the central project function of Spark Clearholme and treated as a larger organisational change.

If you are sure that your change is a local initiative and can be run as part of business as usual, the same business change approach applies as to larger changes, just on a smaller scale. You still need an enthusiastic and effective sponsor (this may be the head of the operational or business unit involved), and each individual affected still needs enough support and information to make the decision to change their ways of working. If this is done, smaller changes implemented locally can be a real success, as they usually offer a workable solution to a genuine problem or opportunity and have the buy-in and ownership of the people most affected by the change.

Creating a compelling vision for the change

Every change initiative needs a vision – a clear and convincing description of what the change is aiming to do and what life will look like once it is in place. This vision is a key engagement tool to enthuse people about the change during the early stages, helping to build support and increase buy-in. It can also be used to keep people positive and focussed when times get tough during implementation. In addition, the vision plays an important role in governing the change by ensuring all activities undertaken contribute to the realisation of the vision. This helps to minimise 'scope creep' – a common phenomenon where the original change initiative slowly expands in an attempt to solve more and more problems.

The vision can be developed at an early stage of the change, as all that is needed are the drivers for the change and an idea of the desired benefits. Details of precise solutions are not needed to create an inspiring, concise, and accessible vision and indeed can easily make the vision too technical and put people off.

Responsibility for developing the vision often falls to the business change manager, but your role here is to facilitate its development by key stakeholders rather than creating it yourself. The vision encapsulates what the change is trying to achieve and therefore needs to be created and owned by those who will be leading the change and who will be responsible for embedding and managing it in the months and years after implementation.

How the development of the vision is facilitated is very much dependent on the organisation and stakeholders involved. Holding a series of workshops with key people is a good way to ensure that all necessary stakeholders are able to offer input into its creation. Some organisations planning significant change even hire external experts to help run these workshops and take key leaders and decision makers away for a number of days to focus solely on this task. If you are not able to engage your key decision makers and leaders through workshops, try creating a draft vision with your project team and any key stakeholders who are willing to engage, and then work individually with all the other relevant leaders and decision makers to ensure that every single one of them is in agreement with what is being suggested. This may involve more than one amendment of the draft vision and can take time, energy, and patience to finalise something that is acceptable to all. However, it is worth investing the time here because if there is not agreement for the vision at this stage, there is a high chance that greater problems will arise as you try to plan and implement the change. How to engage and influence senior stakeholders is discussed further in Chapter 4.

Box 1.3   Real-life example: Burntwood's vision statement for the EDRMS programme

Burntwood's EDRMS will provide better ways of managing electronic information. These will:

- **Help you do your job better:** You can collaborate more easily with others.
- **Save you time:** You can search more easily and find the information you need more quickly.
- **Give you information you can rely on:** You know you have the right version of a document as well as who created it and when.
- **Reduce costs:** You don't keep, and therefore store, any more documents than you need.
- **Protect our service users:** Data will be kept securely and disposed of when no longer needed.
- **Protect us all:** You can provide reliable evidence, stored securely, to explain and justify decisions and meet legal requirements.

This vision is short, easy to read, and inspiring – it describes a future where many day to day issues and irritations are eliminated and clearly describes how the change will benefit individual staff, the organisation, and customers. Notice that it does not go into detail about the specific solutions that will be implemented, namely the EDRMS and associated behaviour changes, but paints a positive picture of the future that everyone can imagine and buy into.

This vision was a key marketing and communications tool for the EDRMS programme and was advertised widely at all stages of the change journey to increase and maintain buy-in. It was also used at key decision points in the programme to check that all planned activities would lead towards the vision. If not, despite however interesting or appealing the suggested activity was, it was classified as scope creep and not taken forward as part of the programme.

Communicating early messages about the change

Anyone involved in the very early stages of a change initiative faces a difficult decision – should the ideas be communicated more widely and if so, how and what should be said? There is often reluctance amongst leaders to communicate about a potential change until there is a high level of certainty that it will go ahead and many of the details of the future are known. This is perfectly understandable, as the initial announcement about a change carries the risk of disturbing staff, affecting motivation, and diverting attention and effort away from business as usual. If communication commences whilst the change idea is still being discussed, people will ask for details which are not yet known, and rumours and speculation about the change will grow quickly. This can cause disruption and unhappiness within the organisation, when the change idea may end up significantly different to the original proposals, or even not happen at all.

However, there are also risks involved with not communicating early about proposed change initiatives. Lack of trust and a feeling that change is being imposed on people can be increased if change is communicated only once it is a 'done deal' and all major decisions have been made. It is also hard to keep secrets in organisations, so it doesn't generally take long for any change ideas discussed behind closed doors to become public knowledge. Rumours, speculation, and conspiracy theories all feed off official silence, and change leaders risk ridicule and cynicism if they come to announce a change they think has been planned in secret only to find out the everyone has known about it for months.

Therefore, like so much else in business change, there is no one right time to communicate about your change. The decision of when to communicate is dependent on a number of factors, including:

- The size and types of impact the change will bring
- Whether the change proposals will be popular
- The number of different solutions being considered
- How much is already widely known about the drivers for change
- How confident and mature the organisation is in dealing with change.

In addition to these factors, Table 1.2 shows some of the advantages and disadvantages of communicating your change idea early. Use this information to help your change leaders decide when to start communicating about your change.

If you do decide to communicate early about your change, there are a few things to bear in mind:

- People will want to ask questions, get involved, and give feedback. Therefore, you need mechanisms in place to manage this. Don't just give out a message about a potential change and leave people with nowhere to go for follow-up.
- You won't have all the answers and detail at this stage, and it is perfectly acceptable to explain this to people. Just make clear what is happening to get the answers, and let them know a date when you will tell them more.
- Explain the drivers for change in early communications to help people see why the change is necessary. If there are no clear drivers, then people will see only 'change for change's sake', and it will be much harder to get buy-in and engagement.
- You will need to update people regularly on how the change idea is progressing. Even if the idea is subsequently dropped, you still need to inform people and explain why. This will increase trust and encourage open and transparent engagement in any future changes.

More information about communicating during change is explored in Chapter 8.

Table 1.2 Advantages and disadvantages of early communications

Advantages	Disadvantages
Early involvement from key stakeholders may result in a better solution as they may have information which can help with planning and designing the future.	If the change will have a major impact, people may be distracted from their day jobs by worrying about the future.
Giving out clear information from official sources combats rumours and speculation which often build the change up to be much worse than it actually is.	Expectations may be raised about a change which eventually does not happen, resulting in cynicism and a lack of confidence in any future changes.
Early indicators of how the change will be received can be gauged, and more time and effort can be given to gaining people's buy-in if necessary.	People will want to ask questions, get involved, and offer opinions which will take time and resources to manage and may detract from the key activities of planning the change.
If people are needed for planning activities, it is easier to engage them and get them released from their business as usual work if everyone knows why.	Organisational resistance in the early stages of a change may result in ideas being dismissed without being examined properly – potentially missing real chances for improvement.
Levels of trust are increased if people are kept informed. Trust is important in implementing successful change, and withholding information makes people feel disempowered, frustrated, and belittled.	If job losses or unpalatable changes are expected, people will begin to look for new roles outside of the organisation. Good staff will go first because they are more employable and you may not have had time to put strategies in place to encourage them to stay.

Box 1.4 Communicating early about a major change in Workout!

Senior leaders at Workout! became aware of a number of drivers for change that were threatening the organisation. Aware that they could not continue to thrive, in fact even survive, as they were, the Head of Employment Services was tasked with investigating current problems and coming up with some early ideas of what a successful future might look like.

Knowing that any future options would require significant changes to the way the organisation was structured and run, the CEO was keen to inform all staff, volunteers, and members of the need for change as early as possible. She used her opening speech at the Workout! annual conference to introduce the idea, focussing on the drivers for the change and reiterating the organisation's key aim of supporting all job seekers in the UK. She admitted that there were no firm ideas of what the change would involve but, knowing how passionate everyone in Workout! was about the aims of the organisation, painted a compelling picture of a future where Workout!

could support more job seekers in a wider variety of ways. She then outlined the timetable for the initial investigation and promised to send out more information in a few months, together with information about how people could become involved. In the meantime, she invited anyone with queries or concerns to contact the Head of Employment Services, who had set up a dedicated email address and allocated time in his schedule to manage any correspondence over the coming weeks.

References and further reading

Balogun, J. and Hope Hailey, V. 2004. *Exploring Strategic Change*. 2nd ed. Harlow: Prentice Hall

Cole, R., King, D. and Sowden, R. 2014. Defining Change. In Smith, R., King, D., Sidhu, R. and Skelsey, D., eds. *The Effective Change Manager's Handbook*. London: Kogan Page, pp. 78–131

Haberburg, A. and Rieple, A. 2012. *Strategic Management Theory and Application*. 3rd ed. Oxford: Oxford University Press

Kotter, John P. 2012. *Leading Change, With New Preface by Author*. Boston: Harvard Business Review Press

Kotter, John P. and Cohen, Dan S. 2002. *The Heart of Change*. Boston: Harvard Business Review Press

Part one

Shaping your change approach

2 Understanding organisational culture

No two organisations and no two change initiatives are ever the same. In order to shape a successful approach to your change, you need to analyse and understand the following four fundamental factors about your particular change situation:

1 The culture of the organisation
2 The type and impact of the change
3 The attitudes and concerns of stakeholders
4 The potential for resistance.

Together, the way these four factors present themselves in your particular situation will enable you to shape your change approach to maximise the potential for your stakeholders to engage with, support, and ultimately choose to adopt and embed your change. The next four chapters explore each of these in turn, and they are brought together in Chapter 6: Shaping Your Change Plan.

The importance of culture in change

An understanding of the culture of your organisation is vital when implementing change. Every organisation has a unique culture, and it will affect your change in two main ways:

1 The impact your change initiative may have on the current culture
2 The impact the current culture may have on your change approach.

The impact of your change initiative on culture

Change will always create a tension with organisational culture because it redefines the way things are done throughout the organisation. The severity of this tension may not be immediately apparent, but you need to understand and tackle it for your change to be truly successful. Changing cultures is hard, so the more the current culture needs to be altered to achieve the benefits of the change, the bigger the change management challenge will be.

The example in Box 2.1 shows how a seemingly straightforward change, implementing a new financial reporting system in an energy company, actually needed the organisation to undertake a major cultural change for the desired benefits to be realised.

Box 2.1   How change initiatives can challenge organisational culture

Following the 2009 UK recession, a large energy company planned a change programme to make the organisation more efficient, cut costs, and demonstrate more value for money in times of austerity. This involved implementing a new financial reporting system which would make all financial decisions within the organisation more transparent.

The organisation had a very strong culture of valuing technical expertise and research and development and were known and celebrated throughout the industry for quality and innovation. Technical experts were very much in charge, and everyone's focus was on developing and building excellent technology with little regard for controlling time or resources. This single-minded pursuit of excellence meant that there was very little interest in or adherence to financial constraints, detailed financial reporting, or strict timetables for delivery.

A move to a more efficient and cost-conscious organisation would challenge this deep-rooted culture, shifting the focus away from quality regardless of cost towards the need to balance quality with financial considerations. Successful implementation and embedding of the change programme would happen only if there was a real focus on cultural and behavioural change, especially amongst the technical experts.

The impact of culture on your change approach

Culture plays a huge part in determining how people behave at work, including how they access and act upon information, influence and are influenced by others, and make decisions and allocate resources. As these are all vital elements of a successful change, your change management approach needs to work within the current culture of your organisation in order for people to feel comfortable engaging in it. A mismatch between culture and the change approach can rapidly isolate people and reduce support for your change, not necessarily because people are uncomfortable with the details of the change itself, but because the culture they are working within does not allow them to behave in the ways you are asking them to during the journey to plan, implement, and embed the change.

The example in Box 2.2 shows how a new business change manager at Burntwood County Council had to reshape his change approach when faced with an organisational culture very different to the one he was used to.

Box 2.2   How culture can affect the change approach

A new business change manager at Burntwood County Council was strug-gling to get to grips with his role. Burntwood had a culture of collabora-tion and collective decision making, with senior leaders disinclined to make decisions which were not supported by their colleagues or staff. Unpopular decisions were often met by considerable resistance throughout the organ-isation and were rarely carried through successfully. The change manager had come from a highly commercial and competitive organisation where decisions were made quickly by individual senior managers and usually accepted by the rest of the organisation without question or resistance.

The change manager was hugely surprised when his first project board meeting at Burntwood was taken up by discussions and no firm decisions were made. This was the complete opposite to his previous organisation and threw his change timetable into disarray. He quickly learned that in order to get decisions about his change made at Burntwood, he had to adapt his approach. The next time that he needed his project board to make a decision, he gave out all the information to the board members in advance and made sure each member had enough time and support to discuss the issues with their colleagues and relevant staff members before attending the meeting. He also arranged to meet each board member separately before the meeting to give them a chance to raise any final thoughts or issues before they were asked to make the decision. Whilst this process took more time and effort than was needed in his former organisation, it enabled his board to feel prepared and confident in mak-ing key decisions about the change and minimised potential resistance from the rest of the organisation.

What is organisational culture?

Organisational culture is a combination of the unspoken values, beliefs, assump-tions, and motivations which shape behaviours and decision making at all levels of an organisation. It is often defined as 'the way we do things around here' (Deal and Kennedy, 1982) or, as often paraphrased, 'the way we do things around here when the boss isn't looking'. Culture plays a very powerful part in determining how leaders, managers, and staff think and act whilst at work, but very few people are aware of its existence, let alone understand how much it influences their behaviour.

Every organisation, from the smallest family business to the largest global corporation, has its own unique organisational culture. Cultures can also vary between different divisions, teams, and geographical areas within organisations. Cultures are very deep rooted and have often been refined and embedded over years, usually subconsciously. Because of this, they are hard to identify and define, and even harder to change.

Sometimes organisational values and value statements can give a clue to culture, but not always. Value statements may be too high level to describe actual cultures in any detail. Sometimes you may find that values are more aspirational statements from leaders than reality on the ground or do not pervade into all parts of the organisation. Whilst it is useful to incorporate values into your change activities and messages where relevant, do not assume they reflect the actual cultures within the organisation without further exploration. Use any cynicism of values as an opportunity to learn more about the real cultures which are developed and strengthened by everyday behaviours and actions across the organisation.

Box 2.3   When culture and values don't match

A UK-wide service organisation had a published organisational value of fairness. When senior leaders described how fairness should look and feel for the organisation they focussed on their customers and the need to treat all customers fairly. However, the same focus on fairness was not apparent within the organisation itself. For example there were discrepancies between employment contracts for staff doing similar jobs in different departments. There was also a history of informal internal promotions, where people whose 'faces fitted' were offered internal career development opportunities. These discrepancies created a high degree of cynicism amongst staff and actually brought to light the real culture within the organisation which was one of favouritism, unofficial power structures, and opaque decision making.

Understanding the culture of your organisation

Given the esoteric nature of organisational culture, it is not always easy or straightforward to analyse and define. However, there are a few tools and techniques which can help you begin to understand the cultures you will be working with in your organisation. Two of these, simple observation and the cultural web, are explored in the following sections.

Simple observation

You can begin to get an idea of the culture of your organisation by simply watching and listening to it at work. The more observations you can gather that point towards certain cultural elements, the stronger the evidence that your analysis is correct. However, making erroneous assumptions about culture is not desirable, so try to validate your findings by discussing them with trusted colleagues and stakeholders to see if they agree with your findings or if they can give you evidence of alternative elements of the organisational culture.

Table 2.1 outlines some things to observe and suggests the type of cultural elements they may indicate.

Table 2.1 Indicating cultural elements through simple observation

Observations	Cultural Elements They May Indicate
Seating arrangements: Is the office open-plan, or do people sit in segmented sections or individual offices? Are there well-used breakout areas or meeting rooms?	Open-plan seating and breakout areas could indicate a collaborative culture, with greater information sharing and group working than found within segmented sections or individual offices.
Management accessibility: Do managers, including senior managers, sit with their teams, or do they have separate offices with closed doors? Are they easily contactable formally and informally?	Managers sitting with teams may indicate a less hierarchical and more informal culture. Look especially at the accessibility of executive managers and the CEO for clues to openness, trust, and transparency.
Dress code: Is this strict and formal or more laid back and casual?	A stricter dress code may indicate a formal and process-led culture, whereas casual dress may indicate more risk taking and innovation.
Language: Is there jargon and terminology specific to the organisation? Do people tell the same stories throughout the organisation?	If people use the same terminology and tell the same stories about the organisation, it could be an indicator of a strong, unified culture where people are all working towards the same aims.
Furnishings: Are the workspaces well decorated and tidy? Are they a comfortable temperature, well lit, clean, and uncluttered?	Pride in the workplace may indicate a culture of pride in work and high levels of motivation and job satisfaction.
Communication: Are there lots of formal meetings and other communications channels, or do teams get together on a more ad-hoc basis? Are there lots of individual conversations in coffee areas or at desks?	A formal communication structure may indicate a culture of process and hierarchy, whereas more informal communications may point towards high levels of personal power and less transparent decision making.

Analysing the culture of Burntwood through simple observation

When the business change manager for the EDRMS programme joined Burntwood County Council, she spent some time observing the organisation at work. Table 2.2 summarises her findings.

From these observations, the business change manager made the following deductions about the culture of Burntwood County Council:

- People are proud of working for Burntwood, shown by the maintenance of the buildings and the pictures of service users and good news stories displayed on the walls.
- There is a feeling of collective culture through language and shared history. However, there is a division between the senior layers of the organisation and the staff shown through different levels of accessibility.

Table 2.2 Simple observation at Burntwood County Council

Observations	Burntwood County Council
Seating arrangements	Most teams sat in open-plan offices along with their team managers. All senior managers had their own offices. The few meeting rooms were often unavailable and most meetings took place informally either in the offices or in the staff canteen.
Management accessibility	All senior managers had their own offices. The CEO and directors had offices on the top floor of the main council building and meetings with them had to be booked at the reception desk found at the entrance to their floor.
Dress code	In the main council building, dress code was formal business wear. In the outlying office buildings, dress code was more informal, with each team deciding what was appropriate depending on their role and relationship with their service users.
Language	Burntwood was full of jargon, abbreviations, and terminology. Each department also had its own local jargon which needed explaining to other staff members when necessary. Key stories from the organisation's history were regularly repeated.
Furnishings	The main council building, which housed the CEO and directors, was an impressive and well-maintained Victorian construction. The outlying offices, where all other services were housed, were modern, purpose-built, and well maintained. Pictures and testimonies from service users, and good news stories about the impact the council has made in the local community, adorn the walls.
Communication	Whilst there were some formal communications channels, none worked effectively. Not everyone read the monthly staff newsletter, and the intranet had very low usage. Dissemination of information cascaded down through the management structure was very dependent on the cooperation of the individual managers. Information was mainly shared on an informal basis, and rumours and speculation were rife. Different departments rarely shared information or worked together to solve problems.

- Information is not evenly or openly shared throughout the organisation, shown by the ineffectiveness of the formal communications channels. Individual power can be increased by forming the right relationships, leaving the rest of the organisation ill-informed and dependent on rumours and speculation.
- Departments are autonomous and see themselves as separate services rather than as part of a larger organisation, as shown by different dress codes, locations, development of local terminology, and reluctance to work together or share information.

She shared these deductions with some colleagues whom she trusted to be truthful and discreet. They confirmed her findings and added their own observations and examples of these cultures in action. The business change manager therefore felt confident that these were key cultures she would need to focus on during her change.

Analysing organisational culture using the cultural web

The best way to really understand an organisational culture is to examine it with the people who work in it every day. However, as culture is so deep rooted, it is often difficult for those working within it to identify and articulate it. The cultural web (Johnson and Scholes, 1988) is a powerful tool which enables people to use their own experiences of working within the organisation to help identify key elements of the culture.

The cultural web consists of six aspects of the way organisations work, which together describe the Paradigm – the culture at the heart of the organisation:

1 **Stories:** the past events and people talked about within the organisation. These stories indicate what behaviours and values the organisation thinks are important.
2 **Rituals and routines:** activities and events which are carried out both formally and informally across the organisation (rituals) and the way things are done in the organisation on a day to day basis (routines).
3 **Symbols:** visual signals such as logos, office layout, furnishings, and dress codes. These reflect the values and cultures of the organisation.
4 **Organisational structure:** the formal structure illustrated by the organisational chart. This is likely to describe where power and key relationships are found within the organisation.
5 **Control systems:** how the organisation is controlled, including financial, quality, and information systems, and how rewards are measured and distributed.
6 **Power structures:** the pockets of real power in the company who play a key role in decision making and direction setting. These groups and individuals will probably reflect the desired cultures and behaviours of the organisation.

Following is an example of how the business change manager at Spark Clearholme ran a workshop with the leaders of the newly merged finance department to help them understand their current culture and target unhelpful behaviour which was hindering their restructure.

Using the cultural web to understand the culture of a newly merged department

The finance department of the newly merged organisation, Spark Clearholme, had been formed by amalgamating the finance teams from the two pre-merger companies, Sparks and Clearholme. A target operating model (the new department structure showing who does what and who reports to whom) had been developed and implemented, but the department was struggling to cope with its workload, despite everyone working harder and harder. Morale was dropping, and there was a serious risk that key individuals across the department would either resign or burn out.

The head of the department was confident that the operating model should be able to manage the workload but was aware that there were behaviours within the department which may be causing the issues. Therefore, she asked the business change manager to help her analyse the culture of the department to understand more about what was driving the unwanted behaviours.

The business change manager held two one-hour workshops with the head of the department and the other ten members of the department's senior leadership team. In the first session, six flip charts were put up on the wall, one for each of the six aspects of the cultural web, and the leaders were asked to populate each flip chart with examples they had experienced and observed within their day to day work. It took a few minutes for the ideas to begin to flow, but by the end of twenty minutes, there were a number of thoughts and examples on each sheet from every delegate. The following are some of these examples:

1   **Stories:** past success of Sparks, Clearholme different and not valued, achieved so much, but so much more to do;
2   **Rituals and routines:** meeting crazy and emails galore, try to achieve too much, everything is a priority – nothing is;
3   **Symbols:** legacy branding, running between meetings, difference in dress codes;
4   **Organisational structure:** lack of delegated authority, 'old' Sparks and Clearholme relationships, governance not defined, and delegated authorities not clear;
5   **Control systems:** reward not obviously linked to success/measures, not confident in addressing underperformance, varying working hours;
6   **Power structures:** all decisions come to leadership team, department head signs off all finances, department head is single point of power.

A facilitated conversation then allowed the senior leaders to discuss their examples in more detail, and cultural themes began to emerge. One theme was 'wasted effort', illustrated by comments such as lack of delegation, not addressing poor performance, and too many meetings and emails. Another theme was 'disjointed', illustrated by poor governance, differing dress codes and working hours, and lack of prioritisation.

The leadership team agreed that both of these themes could be negatively affecting staff and therefore contributing to the work overload. They started to plan how to address and change these cultures to the more desirable ones of 'all effort adds value' and 'a joined up department'. The comments captured during the workshop had outlined some of the practical issues which were contributing to the present cultures and which could be amended, for example standardising dress codes and linking reward to success measures. In addition, the leaders worked with the business change manager to develop a series of change activities to focus on the more intangible challenges such as building the confidence of both senior leaders and their staff in order for successful delegation to take place and increasing all staff's feeling of belonging together in the new department rather than looking back longingly to the old organisations.

What happens next?

Once you have analysed the culture of your organisation, you can use this information to help shape your change approach in the following ways:

- Check whether your proposed change initiative will impact on the current culture and, if so, how. This can be done through the impact assessment described in Chapter 4.
- Incorporate any change initiatives needed to align the organisational culture to your change into your change plan. More on the change plan is given in Chapter 6.
- Ensure that your planned change approach is compatible with the current organisational culture in order for your stakeholders to feel comfortable in engaging with you. Culture will be especially important to take into consideration when you are developing your stakeholder engagement approach (Chapter 3) and the initiatives within your change plan (Chapter 6).

References and further reading

Deal, T. and Kennedy, A. 1982. *Corporate Cultures: Rites and Rituals of Corporate Life*. Harmondsworth: Penguin Books

Johnson, G. and Scholes, K. 1988. *Exploring Corporate Strategy*. Harlow: Prentice Hall

Johnson, G., Whittington, R. and Scholes, K. 2009. *Fundamentals of Strategy*. Harlow: Prentice Hall

Morgan, G. 1998. *Images of Organizations the Executive Edition*. London: Sage

Smith, R. 2014. A Change Management Perspective. In Smith, R., King, D., Sidhu, R. and Skelsey, D., eds. *The Effective Change Manager's Handbook*. London: Kogan Page, pp. 1–77

Thornhill, A., Lewis, P., Millmore, M. and Saunders, M. 2000. *Managing Change: A Human Resource Strategy Approach*. Harlow: Prentice Hall

3   Understanding the impact of change

All change initiatives impact the affected organisation to a greater or lesser extent. In order to plan, implement, and embed your change initiative successfully, you need to understand how the change will impact the organisation and how big this impact will be.

The impact of the change is dependent on three main things:

> **The change initiative itself**, including the number of things changing, the type of things changing, the number of roles and individuals affected, and how different things will be after the change. The bigger the change, the greater the potential impact on the organisation.
>
> **Whether the success of the organisation is dependent on the change** and therefore how much risk is involved if the change runs into problems or fails to deliver what it promises. The more dependent the organisation is on the change, the greater the potential impact.
>
> **The organisation's relationship with managing change**, including how much other change is going on, the organisation's history of managing change, and how confident and mature the organisation is in managing change. The impact of your change will be greater if there are multiple changes happening at the same time, if the organisation has a bad history of managing change, or is not confident or mature in managing change.

Together, these three pieces of analysis will give you an idea of how big an impact your change will have on the organisation. Each is explained in more detail in the following sections.

Understanding the impact of the change initiative

Changing an organisation means asking it to do something differently. To understand the scale and impact of the differences, you need to compare how the organisation works before the change, the current state, and after the change, the future state. The difference between the two states is called the gap and the bigger and more complex the gap, the bigger the scale of the change and the greater the potential impact on the organisation. This comparison is done by undertaking an impact assessment, also known as an impact analysis or gap analysis.

How to undertake an impact assessment

Your organisation might already have an impact assessment template. If not, the McKinsey 7S model (Waterman and Peters, 1982) is a great tool to use. It allows you to examine the impact of your change on seven different aspects of the organisation, as follows:

1   **Strategy:** the plan of how to run the organisation successfully;
2   **Structure:** organisation charts and who reports to whom;
3   **Systems:** formal processes and systems such as IT, rewards, and measurement;
4   **Style:** leadership styles found within the organisation;
5   **Staff:** the general capabilities of the staff;
6   **Skills:** the actual skills and competencies of everyone working for the company;
7   **Shared values:** the culture and core values of the organisation.

The real strength of the 7S model is that it focusses on the impact of the change on behaviours, culture, and values as well as the more tangible areas such as structures and systems. The more esoteric aspects of the organisation are often neglected during change, but focus on them is vital if you want your change to be successful. Even if your organisation has its own method of undertaking an impact analysis, it is worth checking that it covers all the aspects of the 7S model. Your cultural analysis from Chapter 2 will help identify the impact on cultures and behaviours.

In order to carry out an impact assessment using the 7S model, you first need to analyse the differences the change will bring to the seven aspects of your organisation. Do this by listing what happens now – the current state, and what is expected to happen after the change – the future state. Then compare the difference between the two – the gap. Once this is completed, you can decide how significant the gap is for each of the seven aspects. A simple way to do this is to use the scale of high, medium, low, or no change.

You can then use this initial analysis to ascertain the scale and impact of the change on your organisation, by looking at:

> **The number of aspects changing:** how many aspects have a gap between the current and future states;
> **The type of things changing:** the details of what is included in the gaps;
> **The number of people and roles affected:** the details of who is affected by each gap;
> **How different things will be after the change:** how significant the gap is for each of the aspects.

Whilst undertaking your impact assessment, remember that it is purely showing how life is going to be different for the organisation after the change has been made, not about what is going to be put in place to help to transition and support people through the change. It is important to be very clear on the scope of your change and exclude anything that is not directly within your jurisdiction.

Table 3.1 shows the initial analysis for Burntwood's EDRMS.

Table 3.1 Initial 7S analysis for Burntwood's EDRMS

7S Aspect	Current State	Future State	Gap	Size of Gap
Strategy	To produce high quality services To be trusted and transparent	The same	No gap	No change
Structure	Centralised information management team responsible for managing all information	Teams to be responsible for managing their information with support from local information champion	Local information champion role to be created within all teams	Medium
Systems	Shared drives, personal drives, and email accounts used to store electronic information	EDRMS to replace shared drives and personal drives	EDRMS installed and available on all staff machines, shared and personal drives reduced	High
Style	No individual accountability for information management in local teams	Team leaders to be accountable for local information management	New responsibility for team leaders – requiring good management information practices within their teams	High
Staff	Staff generally do not exhibit good information management behaviour	Staff to understand and buy in to the need to manage information well and follow information management policies and processes	Fundamental shift in the way information is thought about and managed throughout the organisation	High
Skills	No pervasive skills, knowledge, or attitudes to managing information safely or well, no knowledge of EDRMS	Skills in using EDRMS and understanding and adhering to information management policies	New skills, knowledge, and attitudes needed to manage information well and use the EDRMS throughout all teams in the organisation	Medium
Shared Values	Autonomy – the desire of individuals and teams to set their own rules and standards	Organisation–wide policies set centrally by subject matter experts and complied with across the organisation	Individuals and teams respect and comply with centrally created policies for collective good	High
	Individual knowledge brings individual power and success	Sharing knowledge will increase success of organisation	Individual achievement comes from working with others to increase success of organisation	
	Administrative tasks are not as important as the 'day job'	Administrative tasks are incorporated into 'day job'	Administrative tasks are everyone's responsibility	

From this analysis, it can be ascertained that the impacts of the change on Burntwood are as follows:

The number of organisational aspects changing: high. Six out of the seven aspects are going to experience some change from the EDRMS.

The type of things changing: high. There will be a new system to store information, new behaviours, and core capabilities; some new roles and responsibilities; and a fundamental shift in the shared values, or culture, of the entire organisation.

The number of people and roles affected: high. All Burntwood staff will be affected to some degree by a change in core capabilities. In addition, all managers will become accountable for information management in their teams, and one team member in each team will need to take on the new role of information champion in addition to their existing work.

How different things will be after the change: high. Six out of the seven areas will experience high or medium levels of change. Three out of the four high levels of change are the areas of behaviour, culture, and values. This suggests significant challenge in implementing and embedding the change.

In summary, the impact assessment shows that the scale of the Burntwood EDRMS programme is large, covering many aspects of the organisation and affecting all staff, and that the change will have a big impact on the whole of the organisation in a variety of tangible, behavioural, and cultural ways.

Is the success of the organisation dependent on the change?

There are two ways the success of the organisation may be dependent on your change:

If the change affects the core activities of the organisation: If the change goes wrong and interferes with these activities, there is a risk that the organisation's short and medium-term success will be threatened.

If the change is contributing to the future strategy of the organisation: If the change fails, there is a risk that the longer term success of the organisation will be threatened.

If the organisation is dependent on your change in either of these ways, the scope of the change is larger and the potential impact significantly higher than if the core business and strategy are not affected. More effort, resources, and planning will be needed to ensure the change is successful and that mitigations are put in place to protect the organisation if something goes wrong.

Table 3.2 shows how dependent some of our example organisations are on their changes and therefore how large the scope and how much potential impact the changes will have.

Table 3.2 Example organisations and their dependency on the success of the change

Change	Dependency	Explanation
Burntwood EDRMS	High	Burntwood runs on information, from creating reports and briefing papers for council members to keeping all service user records complete and up to date. If a failure of the EDRMS means that this information cannot be created and accessed, or the quality of the information deteriorates, the core work of Burntwood will be severely affected.
Mayer & Co E-file	High	The core work of Mayer & Co is to prepare and examine legal cases. After the change is implemented, the only way cases can be accessed is through e-file. If e-file fails, this core business will be severely affected.
Workout! Restructure	High	Workout!'s future strategy depends on a more centralised and transparent way of managing support services for job seekers. Implementing the new employment service areas is a key part of this. If the change fails to be implemented and embedded successfully, the entire future strategy is threatened.
Spark Clearholme Office Move	Medium	The organisation needs to be housed somewhere to carry out its activities. However, there are a number of mitigations that can easily be put in place to enable the core activities to continue during the move should something go wrong.
Spark Clearholme Marketing Campaign Planner	Low	The campaign planner will enable data to be gathered about marketing campaigns but will not affect the actual planning and running of the campaigns which is the core business of the Spark Clearholme marketing teams.

The organisation's relationship with change

No change ever happens in isolation. Your organisation will have lived through many different experiences before your change and will be undertaking many other activities during it. These factors will make a difference to the scope and impact of your change. The main questions to answer to understand your organisation's relationship to change are:

- How much other change is currently going on in the organisation?
- What is the history of implementing change in the organisation?
- How confident and mature is the organisation in leading change?

How much other change is currently going on in the organisation?

For organisations to change only one thing at a time is rare. Normally there are several related and unrelated changes occurring simultaneously. You will know about some of the changes, but some you may not be aware of unless you stumble upon them during your own change activities.

It is important to take other changes into account when planning your change for a number of reasons, including:

- The cumulative effect of many changes may mean your change feels more problematic for some stakeholders than it would do in isolation. If the same people are being targeted by a number of significant changes at the same time, they may not have any emotional energy left to cope with your change.
- If your change leaders and decision makers are also focussing on other changes happening across the organisation, they may have limited time and energy for your change and place less importance on its success.
- Your users may have already allocated all their available time and resources to other changes. For example they may already be attending training sessions for other change initiatives, nominating champions and super users, spending time preparing for implementation, and focussing on new ways of working. This may leave very little time for them to invest in your change.
- Simultaneous communications about lots of separate changes will confuse and annoy users and lead to information overload. Important messages about your change may become lost in a mass of change communications and not be read or responded to.
- Users affected by more than one change will not see them as different entities. They will ask you for help and information about other changes they are experiencing and will quickly become frustrated and confused if they have to go to lots of different places for support.
- Users affected by more than one change will become very irritated if they are asked to duplicate activities, for example providing the same information about their teams or attending two different training sessions in proximity to each other.
- If you are very unlucky, you may find yourself in a situation where different changes are giving out competing messages about desired cultural and behavioural changes. Not only will this confuse and irritate users but it will also jeopardise the success of all the change. It can also cause conflict between organisational leaders and decision makers and make it incredibly difficult for your change to succeed.

Box 3.1   When two major change initiatives conflicted in desired cultures and behaviours

At the same time as Burntwood's EDRMS programme was investigating how best to improve the council's information management practices, the technology department was developing its strategy for the future.

Separately, both initiatives investigated current best practice in their subjects and recommended solutions which, in isolation, would give the best outcomes for each of the challenges they were facing.

When the two solutions were compared, however, there was a conflict between how users were being asked to behave. The benefits of the EDRMS programme would be realised only if users took the time to file information in carefully managed electronic storage areas and trawl these regularly to get rid of as many documents as possible. The success of the IT strategy was dependent on minimising effort by keeping all electronic information in mass storage with minimal filing and deletion activities, locating necessary documents through a sophisticated search engine.

It quickly became obvious that it would be impossible to ask users to manage their information in both ways, so to continue with both changes would lead to confusion and failure. It was up to the senior leaders and decision makers within the organisation to decide on a way forward which would best serve the needs of the organisation as a whole rather than looking at the benefits of either change initiatives as a separate entity.

Once you have an idea of what other changes are happening alongside your change, you will be able to ascertain how they may affect the impact of your change. To reduce undesirable impacts, you can collaborate with other change initiatives and run joint activities, for example:

- Coordinating the changes to minimise the cumulative impacts on the organisation;
- Joining up engagement activities to ensure a coherent and manageable approach for users;
- Sending out joint communications to minimise information overload;
- Developing a collaborative support model so it is easy for users to access support for any of the changes they are experiencing.

What is the history of implementing change in the organisation?

Just as your change will not be the only one happening at any one time, neither will your initiative be the first change your organisation has ever attempted. Individual stakeholders may also have experienced change whilst working in previous organisations. These earlier experiences will affect how people react to and interact with your change.

Positive experiences will increase confidence in your change. People will be more willing to engage with you and give time and resources to help, and they will be more likely to believe that the change will succeed and bring benefits.

Negative experiences will lead to suspicion and cynicism about your change. If individuals and teams have experienced unsuccessful change in the past, they will not see the point in investing time in your initiative, as they will expect it to end in failure. If people are used to having change forced on them with little or no involvement, they will be reluctant to engage in your change, as they will have no confidence that they will be listened to.

Mayer & Co E-file
Change Pledge

Good change happened when...

- We understood why the change needed to happen
- People listened to our questions and concerns
- There was early engagement
- There was learning from previous mistakes
- Our expectations about the change were managed
- The change led to a more unified service

Bad change happened when...

- Decision points took too long then change was rushed through
- There was ambiguity, causing anxiety of the unknown
- It was change for change's sake
- There was a lack of engagement
- We were consulted but there was no action or feedback as a result
- There was a lack of training and support

Therefore we pledge to...

Make sure the need for change is clear
Ensure there is enough time to plan the change properly
Engage early and frequently about the change
Be clear on what is happening and what is expected from you
Consult, listen to concerns, and be clear on how we will deal with feedback
Ensure there is enough training and support for everyone
Check frequently on how people are feeling about the change

Figure 3.1 The Mayer & Co e-file change pledge

The best way to learn about the organisation's history with change, and to begin to build trust and confidence in people who have suffered bad change, is to ask people to tell you about their experiences. Book a meeting room for an hour, supply some coffee and biscuits, and invite users to come and tell you about their positive and negative experiences of change. People tend to incline towards the negative, so you may have to encourage them to recall positive experiences as well, but you should come out of the workshop with a good idea of the history of change within the organisation and some individual experiences of change in other organisations. You will also come away with lots of suggestions of what and what not to do during your change to make it successful.

A powerful next step is to develop this feedback into a change pledge (see Figure 3.1) – a public promise from you to your users about how you will manage your change. This can be an effective way of building trust, especially if you ask your users to call you to account if the pledge is broken. If you are going to create a pledge, however, you and your change leaders must be confident that you can deliver all your promises. If you pledge that the change will be managed well and then let people down, they will be even more cynical next time.

How confident and mature is the organisation in leading change?

Organisations which are confident and mature in delivering change generally deliver change well – they have a good capability in change. The better the capability within the organisation, the less impact your change will have, purely because people know what to expect, and what is expected of them.

There are four key roles which contribute to a good organisational capability in change:

1   **Change leaders:** They have knowledge of what change feels like to implement and understand the need to create and maintain a compelling vision. They understand how to make decisions during change and ensure that all initiatives are compatible and contribute to the organisation's overall strategy and vision of the future. They are confident in leading the organisation through the uncertainty and risks that change brings.

2   **Middle managers:** They know how to balance the pressures of maintaining business as usual whilst investing enough time and resource in change. They understand the need for organisational change and engage positively with change initiatives to ensure local information and ideas are contributed. They take the lead in managing their staff through change and ensuring the change is implemented and embedded successfully in their areas.

3   **Staff making the changes:** They will have confidence and trust in the organisation's ability to manage change. They recognise the need for organisational change and understand the emotional instability and short-term effect on productivity that change often brings. They are willing to engage in the change by undertaking preparation activities, trying things out, feeding back on successes, and suggesting improvements.

4   **Teams working on the change:** Support teams such as HR, Learning and Development, Internal Communications, and Technology are often needed to help with change initiatives. Experienced teams will understand and manage the specific demands that change activities place on them and fully engage in supporting the change alongside their business as usual roles.

If you are planning to implement a change in an organisation where those in the key roles do not exhibit these behaviours, the impact of your change will be greater. Not only will additional time and resources be needed to support those in the key roles, but also a lack of organisational change capability will increase the chances of resistance and lack of engagement for your change which will require extra change interventions to overcome.

What happens next?

The analysis you have carried out during this chapter will show you the level of impact your change will have on your organisation due to the impact of the change initiative itself, how dependent the organisation is on the change, and the organisation's relationship with managing change.

Depending on how high these impacts are, you will need to develop change initiatives to deal with each of them. These will need to be put in your change plan alongside the initiatives needed to engage stakeholders (Chapter 4) and manage any potential resistance (Chapter 5). More about developing the change plan can be found in Chapter 6.

References and further reading

Cameron, E. and Green, M. 2009. *Making Sense of Change Management.* 2nd ed. London: Kogan Page

Perkins, C. 2014. Change Impact. In Smith, R., King, D., Sidhu, R. and Skelsey, D., eds. *The Effective Change Manager's Handbook.* London: Kogan Page, pp. 258–289

Waterman, R. and Peters, T. 1982. *In Search of Excellence.* New York: Collins

4　Understanding stakeholder engagement

Stakeholders are anyone with a 'stake' or interest in your change. They consist of everyone involved in or affected by your change and whose actions will ultimately determine its success. Understanding and engaging with your stakeholders is a fundamental part of the business change role, and a detailed knowledge of your stakeholders will play a significant part in how you shape and execute your change approach.

Stakeholder engagement is dynamic and complex. Every single one of your stakeholders is a unique and independent person, a bundle of motivations, emotions, assumptions, imperfections, and idiosyncrasies – just like you and me. They will have their own opinions on your change and, depending on how much power they hold within the organisation, may have the potential to 'make or break' it. The way they respond to your change can depend on a number of obvious or obscure reasons and they can be heavily influenced by, and influence, other stakeholders. In addition, their opinions, enthusiasm, and actions can vary significantly over time – your stakeholders are continually changing the shape of their interest, support, and resistance to your change.

This means that engaging with stakeholders through your change is like embarking on a chess game with many players, each playing to slightly different rules. It is vitally important to understand who your stakeholders are; how much power they have; whether they support your change; their drivers, assumptions, and opinions; who influences them; and how they are likely to act towards your change. You then need to keep close to their every move and try to engage with them positively throughout the change to increase your chances of success.

You will never find two identical stakeholders in the same organisation, let alone in different organisations, and therefore your stakeholder engagement activities will never be the same twice. An in-depth understanding of your stakeholders is a key tool to successfully shaping your business change approach for each change initiative you tackle.

Identifying your stakeholders

The most obvious stakeholders are those affected by your change – your end users or customers. However, there are many other people who also need to be

Leading the change	Making the change happen	Making the change successful
• Make decisions about the change: what is going to change, how it will change, and when the change will happen • Provide resources, including money and people, to plan, implement, and embed the change • Ensure the change has leadership support and prioritisation • Help solve any problems that may arise during the change	• Build the new products and design the associated activities needed for the change • Undertake practical activities to put the change into the organisation • Provide support, resources, and expertise to make the change happen	• Ensure the changes are workable for all the different groups of people affected • Ensure everyone affected knows what is happening and what they will need to do differently • Make any necessary changes; participate in the change; feed back thoughts, suggestions, and best practice; and not resist • Ensure the change is embedded and the benefits of the change are realised

Figure 4.1 Stakeholder groups and key activities

involved in your change. Figure 4.1 shows three different groups of stakeholders for change initiatives and lists some of their key activities.

Once you start working through the above list even small, contained changes start to involve a lot of stakeholders. Large changes can involve significant amounts of individuals and groups – 50 to 100 key stakeholders and stakeholder groups are not unusual in sizeable changes, and you can expect to work with even more during very significant or complex change.

There are various ways to identify your stakeholders. One tried and tested technique is to hold a workshop with project team members and business representatives. Everyone writes down all the stakeholder names they can think of on separate sticky notes and then takes turns to post the sticky notes on a flip chart, eliminating duplication and adding more names as they discuss.

Box 4.1   Running a stakeholder identification workshop for Burntwood EDRMS

Early on in the planning of the change, a workshop was held with EDRMS programme staff and one representative from each of the technology and information management department and from operational departments. The workshop lasted one hour, with everyone writing names on sticky notes and then taking turns to put on a flip chart, discounting any duplicates and adding any more which came to mind during the activity. The stakeholders were then divided into the three categories relating to the activities they would be carrying out during the change and the Burntwood EDRMS stakeholder diagram produced, as shown in Figure 4.2.

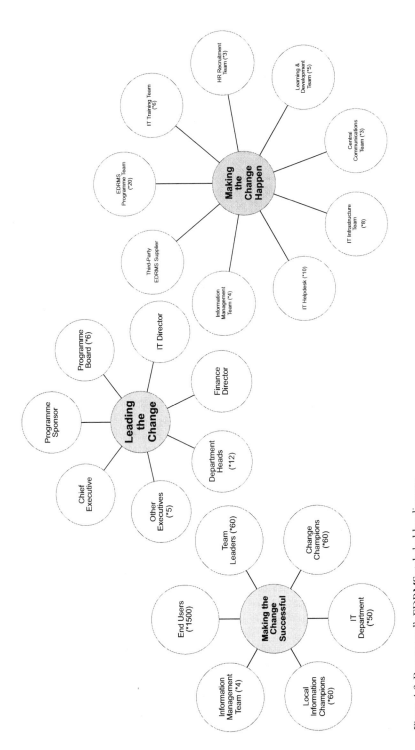

Leading the Change
- Programme Board (*6)
- Programme Sponsor
- Chief Executive
- Other Executives (*5)
- Department Heads (*12)
- Finance Director
- IT Director

Making the Change Happen
- EDRMS Programme Team (*20)
- IT Training Team (*6)
- HR Recruitment Team (*3)
- Learning & Development Team (*5)
- Central Communications Team (*3)
- IT Infrastructure Team (*8)
- IT Helpdesk (*10)
- Information Management Team (*4)
- Third-Party EDRMS Supplier

Making the Change Successful
- Team Leaders (*60)
- Change Champions (*60)
- IT Department (*50)
- Local Information Champions (*60)
- Information Management Team (*4)
- End Users (*1500)

Figure 4.2 Burntwood's EDRMS stakeholder diagram

How does it feel to do a stakeholder identification workshop?

You may find yourself becoming increasingly agitated as you go through this exercise and your list of stakeholders grows and grows. At some point, you may well find yourself thinking 'I will never have the time to engage with all these people, considering everything else I have to do!'

It is important not to panic at this point. As explained earlier, even small changes require the input of lots of people. However, you will find when you start to map your stakeholders (as described in the next section) that the most powerful stakeholders are easily identifiable. These are the ones you need to engage with most throughout the change, and you may find that you can cluster less powerful stakeholders, who will not need as intense engagement, into larger groups with similar concerns and engagement needs. Whilst effective stakeholder engagement is time consuming and resource intensive, you should find that you can manipulate your original list into a manageable plan. If you can't, you can at least use your stakeholder analysis to help build a compelling case for more resources to manage your stakeholders.

During your identification workshop, you may also start hearing stories about individual stakeholders who are prominent within the organisation in some way. Either legendary tales of those whose heroic feats have saved the organisation from disaster in the past, or horror stories of more notorious stakeholders with renowned reputations as difficult, obstructive, and stubborn. Whilst it is great to hear about the positive stakeholders, especially if they are supportive of your change, the stories of notoriety may leave you unsettled and wondering whether your change is doomed to failure before it has begun. Again, don't panic. Getting bad experiences out in the open can be cathartic for attendees, and sharing stories can help build strong relationships within your own change team. Remember that you are only hearing one side of the story, so flag the names to remind you to do some more research before making up your own mind on the best ways to engage with them.

Box 4.2 Identifying prominent personalities for Burntwood EDRMS

During the EDRMS stakeholder identification workshop, stories were told about three key stakeholders who held a lot of power within the organisation and whose reactions to the change so far had been noticeable:

IT Director: Stories were told of how she regularly voices her displeasure with the EDRMS, making it clear that she would prefer a different solution which would fit better with her ambitious (and yet to be agreed upon) technology strategy. Incidents where she had publicly humiliated adversaries were relayed. The overwhelming reaction amongst attendees towards her was fear and frustration – she was a very difficult person to deal with, remote and untouchable.

Head of Adult Services: Sitting in a relatively powerful position, this departmental head has been very vocal about his opposition to the programme. Notoriously difficult to please, difficult to manage and influential, the attendees saw him as a very tricky stakeholder with some as yet unidentified issues with the programme.

One very powerful and well-respected stakeholder, the **Chief Executive,** was identified as being positive towards the change. Stories were told of him raising information management issues in key meetings and presentations, his informal support for the programme, and his very good relationship with the programme sponsor. The overall feeling amongst attendees was that he is highly respected, calm, and approachable and could be a very powerful ally during the change.

A few things to bear in mind when doing a stakeholder identification exercise

- The only way to identify all your stakeholders is to consult with a range of people who are familiar with different aspects of your organisation and the change initiative. Don't try to identify all stakeholders on your own as you will never know enough to capture everyone by yourself.
- Even after completing your original identification exercise, continue to ask people who else should be involved as you carry out your engagement activities. This will help you pick up any stakeholders not initially identified and make you aware of new stakeholders as the change initiative develops.
- Some stakeholders will play more than one role in your change. For example the information management team is both part of the delivery team and end users for the Burntwood EDRMS. This is normal and means that you have to engage with these stakeholders in either or both their roles where appropriate.
- People regularly move roles and leave organisations. Keep your stakeholder list up to date and remember that any alteration of personnel in key stakeholder positions may result in a different balance of power and subsequent amendment to your engagement approach.
- Make sure you include everyone who will be affected by your change. It is easy to forget that change can impact in wider and more subtle ways than is immediately apparent. Think through every aspect and impact of your change to make sure no-one is missed out. The impact assessment described in Chapter 3 will help with this.

Box 4.3 The risk of not identifying all stakeholders

The scope of Spark Clearholme's office move was to relocate staff from three out of the four original buildings into the new offices. The staff in the fourth building specialised in a line of work which was to be discontinued by the merged company within the next two years. As the lease on their current building could be extended for that time, it was decided that they would stay where they were.

As they were not physically moving location, the staff remaining in the fourth building were not obvious stakeholders for the change. In reality, however, the move had a big impact on them. They needed to know the details of where their colleagues were moving to, but more importantly, they began to feel very excluded and ignored. In order to raise excitement and buy-in about the move there had been a lot of organisation-wide communication about the benefits of the move, and this group had been recipients along with their colleagues. Not only did these communications make them feel they were missing out, they were also a reminder that they would shortly have no place in the organisation. Morale dropped and performance began to suffer. Once this was bought to the business change manager's attention, she quickly arranged some specific change interventions for this group to improve morale and make them feel more included.

Stakeholder mapping

Once you have identified your stakeholders, you need to understand how important they are in relation to your change. Mapping stakeholders onto an interest/influence matrix will help you to understand how much power each individual or group holds and how much interest they have in your change. This exercise is very useful for highlighting key stakeholders who can help realise your change and those who will try to block it.

Undertaking a stakeholder mapping exercise

For each stakeholder or stakeholder group you have identified for your change, you need to decide the following:

- **How interested they are in the change:** how supportive or worried they are about the change or how much do they stand to gain or lose. Interest tends to be higher for stakeholders who are more impacted by the change.
- **How influential they are regarding the change:** whether the stakeholder has the power to cause trouble and derail your change or remove barriers and actively move your change towards success.
- **What your stakeholder's attitude to the change is:** whether they are positive, negative, or neutral about your change.

As with the identification exercise, you can hold a workshop with trusted colleagues to develop your stakeholder map. Draw the matrix on some flip chart paper and put sticky notes with the names of your stakeholders on the correct

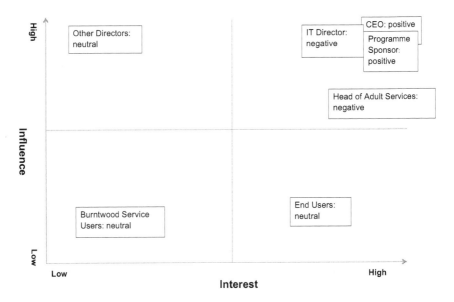

Figure 4.3 Stakeholder matrix for Burntwood's EDRMS (excerpt)

part of the grid. You will probably have some discussion about where the stake-holders should go, especially around 'interest'. Don't worry about being too accurate, as you can always refine where you position your stakeholders as you get to know them. The key thing here is to get a high level understanding of where people are currently sitting regarding your change.

Figure 4.3 shows an excerpt of the stakeholder matrix developed for Burn-twood's EDRMS.

What the mapping exercise will tell you

Mapping stakeholders onto the interest/influence grid starts to give you an idea of how important they are for your change and whether they are in the right place to assist in your change or whether they have positioned themselves so that they can hinder it should they chose to do so.

As you can see from the EDRMS example in Figure 4.3, the matrix is divided into four quadrants. Stakeholders sitting in the different quadrants, and with differing attitudes, will all respond differently to your change. Typical behaviours for each of the quadrants and suggested responses are described in the following sections.

Top right quadrant: high interest and high influence

This is where your most powerful stakeholders should be sitting, including change sponsors, operational leaders whose teams will be affected, senior leaders, decision makers, and those who are resourcing your change.

Positive stakeholders in this quadrant are very powerful allies and can be a great help in overcoming any barriers and problems that may arise during your change. For Burntwood's EDRMS, both the CEO and the programme sponsor sit in the top corner of this quadrant and with a positive attitude to the change. This is where they need to be, and the stakeholder engagement approach for them throughout the change focusses on keeping them there.

Negative stakeholders who sit in this quadrant can cause a lot of problems. In Burntwood, the IT Director sits here. The change impacts directly on her own work – her IT strategy – so she is very interested in the change, and her position in the organisation coupled with her high levels of personal power gives her the influence to cause problems if she wants to. Therefore, future engagement aims to move her attitude from negative to either neutral or (if possible) positive, and at the same time decrease either her interest, or her influence, or both.

Top left quadrant: high influence and low interest

Stakeholders who sit here can be dangerous because of the influence they command within the organisation. Providing nothing happens within your change to make them interested, they will not help or hinder in any major way. However, if something happens to ignite their interest, they will move straight into the top right quadrant and suddenly become a very key player.

For Burntwood's EDRMS, Other Directors sit as a group high in this quadrant. These are members of the organisation's executive team who are not currently impacted by the EDRMS programme. Their engagement approach aims to move their current neutral attitude to positive, so that if something happens to increase their interest in the change, for example the scope widens and they are suddenly impacted, they will move to the top right quadrant as strong supporters of the change.

Bottom right quadrant: high interest and low influence

This is an interesting place for stakeholders to sit. Their low influence means that they have very little power to help or hinder your change, but their high interest means that they can be very time consuming to deal with. If they are negative about your change, they will seek reassurance and answers to problems, and if they are positive they will want to become involved, offer suggestions, and try things out. A good engagement approach could consist of trying to reduce the interest or increase the attitude of the negative stakeholders and increase the influence of the positive stakeholders, as they could be useful allies due to their natural enthusiasm for your change.

Groups of end users are often put into this quadrant. They are obviously interested in the change, as it will affect the way they work but are often seen as not having very much influence. If they are negative, however, they may work hard to increase their levels of influence in order to block or derail your change. This could be done by negatively influencing someone who has more power than them (in Burntwood, the IT Director would be a willing recipient of unhappy users' complaints), covert resistance such as sabotage, or simply through the power of many – if the majority of your end users decides not to adopt the new ways of working, they will be hugely influential in how successful or otherwise your change ends up. Therefore, their engagement activities focus on moving their attitude to positive and then increasing their influence.

Bottom left quadrant: low interest and low influence

There is very little you need to do with these stakeholders unless you have enough resource to engage with them. Whilst it would be nice to keep them informed, you will probably find you are spending all your time dealing with stakeholders in the other quadrants, so just keep watch over these people and make sure that they do not increase either their interest or influence due to changes in your change initiative or in the wider organisational environment. For example the Burntwood Service Users can remain in this quadrant, as they have very little interest or influence over internal administrative changes within the council. The danger will come if there are ever any problems with the security or operation of the EDRMS which either puts their data at risk or impacts the service they receive from the council. In either case, both their interest and influence will increase dramatically, and they will become key players.

Getting to know your stakeholders

Now that you have a clearer idea of who your stakeholders are and where they sit in relation to your change, you need to think about how best to engage with them. In order to plan successful engagement activities, you need to build up a rich picture of each of your stakeholders and stakeholder groups as living entities. Try to really 'get under the skin' of your stakeholders and begin to understand their drivers, motivations, interests, history, influences, and ambitions. You can then use this information to build strong relationships with each individual, understand why they are acting and reacting to your change in their differing ways, and start to anticipate their potential moves during your forthcoming chess game of change.

You can build this picture through a number of activities:

- **Get to know your stakeholders:** Start your engagement by meeting them for an informal introductory chat and a coffee. Go prepared with a few open questions and listen to them talk. You will learn a lot about them through the topics they choose to focus on, the examples they use, the stories they tell, and the enthusiasms and concerns they have about your change. Give them some information about yourself too, so they can understand more about you, and you will begin to build a trusting relationship.
- **Ask people who know them:** This may include your change team colleagues, project board and sponsors, their direct reports, team members, and

personal assistants. Be careful to ask only people you trust. There is a fine line between researching your stakeholders in order to better engage with them and indulging in rumours and office gossip.

- **Undertake desk research:** Try to find out what your stakeholders have been involved in in the past. What change initiatives have they initiated, sponsored, supported, or resisted? What boards or decision-making groups are they involved in? Who reports to them, and who do they report to?

- **Find out about their life outside of the organisation:** Areas include their career history, where else they have worked, and even what outside interests they have. It is amazing how meaningful relationships can develop through shared interests such as sport or music, mutual acquaintances, or even a sympathetic understanding of difficult commuter routes or the challenges of coping with aging parents and uncommunicative teenagers.

Developing a stakeholder engagement plan

Having built up a deep understanding of your stakeholders, you can use this information to put together a comprehensive stakeholder engagement plan.

The stakeholder engagement plan outlines the current and desired position of your stakeholders on the interest/influence matrix, the engagement activities you will undertake to help them move to the desired position, and the measures which will show that you have been successful. You will probably not have the time and resources to engage comprehensively with all your stakeholders, so concentrate on those with the most power – the ones you really need support from to make the change work.

Table 4.1 shows an excerpt from the Burntwood EDRMS stakeholder engagement plan showing the engagement approach for three key stakeholders. Note that only one of the stakeholders is being engaged by the business change manager. Due to the CEO's seniority, the programme sponsor led on his engagement activities, and the IT Director was engaged by a respected IT manager whom she had seconded onto the EDRMS programme to oversee the technology development work.

Once your engagement plan is developed, it will need to be continually updated, refined, and reshaped. Each engagement activity will elicit a response from the stakeholder, and subsequent activities may need to be amended, depending on this response.

For example at one of the quarterly catch-ups between the CEO and the programme sponsor, the CEO raised some concerns with the amount of time being proposed to train end users on the new system. He was worried about how users would feel about undertaking a long training session and had some concerns about the potential impact the training may have on business as usual activities. It was important to resolve this quickly; otherwise, there was a risk that the CEO would no longer feel so positive about the change.

Table 4.1 Burntwood EDRMS stakeholder engagement plan (excerpt)

Stakeholder	Current Position	Desired Position	Engagement Activities	Success Measures
CEO	Very high interest and influence Positive attitude	Maintain position and attitude	One-to-one update by the programme sponsor once a quarter Interview for intranet – why the EDRMS programme is good for the organisation Ask if his office could be a pilot	Happy with how the programme is going – no issues or concerns Accepts interview request and participates Accepts office as pilot, participates and feedbacks for pilot review
IT Director	High interest and influence Negative attitude	High interest and medium influence Neutral attitude	Decrease influence to block change by embedding EDRMS programme in organisational plans and budgets Regular meetings with trusted IT colleague seconded on project to manage key interests and concerns Identify where programme will benefit IT department – buy-in of key IT managers and direct reports to move Director from negative to neutral attitude	EDRMS programme included in organisational plans and budgets Meetings set up and go ahead, Director's concerns made apparent and discussed openly Key IT managers and direct reports bought into project and reporting up to Director how it will benefit them
Head of Adult Services	High interest, medium influence Negative attitude	High interest and low influence Neutral attitude	One-to-one meeting to find out what his concerns are Agree plan to address those concerns Meet regularly for updates Share his concerns and how they are being addressed with other key stakeholders	Clear understanding of concerns Practical action plan to address concerns Increasing positivity Less feedback from other stakeholders about how they are concerned because of his concerns

Therefore, the business change manager built two more engagement activities into the engagement plan to resolve this:

1   A review of the proposed training plan to see if the classroom-based training session could be reduced, and other support increased to ensure users were still fully trained whilst receiving less classroom-based training.
2   A demo of the system was held for all senior stakeholders, including the CEO, to show them the key features of the system and the potential benefits. This increased buy-in and positivity for the project and also showed the CEO that in order for the system to be used properly, users needed to be given the time to train and learn the system properly.

These two activities resulted in an agreed amount of classroom-based training for each user, less than originally planned but enough to ensure everyone would be properly trained and supported, and full support for the training plan from the CEO.

What happens next?

Incorporate your stakeholder engagement plan into your change plan and use your stakeholder analysis to develop any other relevant change initiatives to increase buy-in and reduce negativity towards your change. More information on developing the change plan is given in Chapter 6.

References and further reading

Ackermann, F. and Eden, C. 2011. *Making Strategy: Mapping Out Strategic Success*. Thousand Oaks: Sage
Handy, C. 1993. *Understanding Organizations*. 4th ed. London: Penguin Books
Kotter, John P. 1996. *Leading Change*. Boston: Harvard Business School Press
Mayfield, P. 2014. Stakeholder Strategy. In Smith, R., King, D., Sidhu, R. and Skelsey, D., eds. *The Effective Change Manager's Handbook*. London: Kogan Page, pp. 172–209

5 Understanding resistance

The previous three chapters have helped you develop a good understanding of your organisational culture, the scope and impact of your proposed change, and the stakeholders you will be working with. Just before you turn your attention to developing the change plan, we need to examine resistance to change.

Resistance is a phenomenon closely associated with business change, and it is often part of the business change manager's role to 'manage resistance' or develop a 'resistance management plan'. Before you can decide how to approach this, you need to understand why people may choose to resist change and how to recognise that resistance is happening.

Is resistance normal?

Humans are not naturally opposed to change. If we were, there would never be the phenomenal advances in technology, science, philosophy, and the arts which play such an integral part in our development as a species. Neither would any individual progress their career or relationships, move house, have children, learn new skills, enjoy hobbies, or achieve pretty much anything at all.

However, it is not unusual to experience resistance when attempting organisational change. This is often explained away with the statement 'people just don't like change'. Such a simplistic attitude is in direct conflict with evidence from history and is very dangerous when working in change, as it normalises resistance, regarding it as something that is inherent in individuals and therefore is to be expected and managed.

If people don't automatically oppose change in other spheres of life, why is resistance such a big part of organisational change? One answer could be that, whilst resistance to change is not inherent in us as individuals, we do all have a very strong, inbuilt sense of self-preservation. When change threatens this in some way and we perceive a risk to our safety, security, or well-being, we fight back. Often, the only way to do this in organisations is through undertaking some form of resistance.

Most organisational changes do not threaten individual self-preservation to any great degree. However, bad practices in the way that change is planned, communicated, and implemented frequently results in people feeling threatened and responding with resistant behaviours. Therefore, resistance is not an action carried out by affected individuals because they 'don't like change', but a reaction by people who feel threatened by decisions and actions carried out by those managing the change. The responsibility lies firmly with us – if we manage our changes well, people will not feel threatened and resistance will be minimised. Manage it badly and resistance will increase exponentially.

Common causes of resistance

So what can you do differently to minimise resistance to your change? Rosabeth Moss Kanter, a professor of business at Harvard Business School, has undertaken some research into why people resist organisational change (Kanter, 2012). Table 5.1 shows the ten common reasons for resistance she identified and suggests some practical actions you can take to prevent them. It is interesting to note that only the last of the reasons, 'sometimes the threat is real', which concerns the content of the change itself. The other nine reasons are created by the way the change is planned and managed – activities which you should be able to influence and control.

How to recognise when people are resisting

As a business change manager, your aim is to shape your change approach to eliminate resistance as much as possible. However, you may find yourself in a situation where it is simply not possible to remove all the common reasons for resistance. For example there may be a very tight deadline for implementation, meaning you can't fully involve and prepare people for the change, or there are a number of interlinked changes that all need to happen at once, increasing pressure on users. In these cases, you will need to prepare yourself for a certain level of resistance.

The following three common forms of resistance are examined, along with tips on how to recognise they are happening and some suggestions of what you can do to minimise the resistance as much as possible.

People being very vocal in their objections to the change, including

- Constantly raising objections at meetings and workshops;
- Contacting you, your project colleagues, and your change leaders with multiple complaints about the change;
- Raising their objections and unhappiness with their managers, colleagues, and teams.

Vocal resistors may have one or two very clear objections, but generally they are negative about all aspects of the change, finding problems with every suggestion, activity, and communication.

Table 5.1 Common causes of resistance

Reason for Resistance	Preventions	Example
Loss of control: People often feel they lose autonomy, self-determination, and control over their territory when faced with changes proposed and led by someone else.	Increase the sense of control and ownership by involving people in the planning, decision making, and design and implementation of the change where possible. Allow lots of opportunities for feedback and be seen to be acting on it.	**Burntwood EDRMS:** When choosing the software to manage the organisation's information, two well-respected representatives were chosen from within the organisation to offer input in to the decision-making process on behalf of the users.
Excessive uncertainty: Change can feel like a big leap into the unknown – unsettling and risky with the potential for all sorts of problems to arise.	Try to create a sense of safety where possible – share what you know about the future as and when it becomes clear. Give clear timetables and plans for how the change is going to be implemented. Let people know how they are going to be supported through the change and where to go for help.	**Mayer & Co E-file:** Each affected team attended a demo of the new e-file system where they were shown how it worked and were given a chance to explore as a team how it would affect them. They were also given very clear timelines on how the system would be implemented and where they could go for support.
Change takes people by surprise: Change planned in secret and then imposed on people with very little notice will threaten people's sense of security and well-being.	Communicate what is being planned as soon as you can. Seek input and involve people where possible in planning the change. Give people information about the change early enough that they can get used to the idea and prepare for the impacts of the change.	**Spark Clearholme Office Move:** From very early in the planning stage, users were kept informed with regular updates on the intranet, tours of the new building, and a demonstration layout in the current reception area to help people to adjust to the new layout.
Everything seems to be changing: Too many differences at once can feel overwhelming and reduce people's ability to engage in individual changes.	Try to schedule change so no user group is affected by too much change at once. Focus on what is really important to change and minimise other changes being made at the same time.	**Spark Clearholme Merger:** A huge amount of change was needed to integrate the two old companies into one. Detailed analysis was carried out to show when each change was impacting each department, and changes were planned in conjunction with each other to make sure no department was undertaking too many changes at once.

Issue	Action	Case example
Loss of face: There will always be someone within the organisation associated with instigating and championing the current ways of working. The need for change is an inference of failure for these people and can be demoralising and humiliating.	Protect these people's dignity and reduce personal blame by being very clear about the drivers for the current change. Focus on what is still working and will be taken forward. Recognise and celebrate past achievements driven by the old ways of working.	**Spark Clearholme Finance Dept Restructure:** Work on the cultural change needed for new finance department focused around a number of cultures that already worked. Any changes needed were described as building on and enhancing these rather than viewing the whole current culture as broken and needing to be rebuilt.
Concerns about competence: People may not feel confident that they can actually learn and adapt to new ways of working. They worry they may feel stupid and incompetent, they are not good enough to do their jobs, or their skills will become obsolete.	Provide lots of support, training, reassurance, and time whilst people learn new skills and behaviours. Be clear on what skills and competencies are needed for the future. Listen to people's concerns and mitigate them with extra support where possible.	**Mayer & Co E-file:** All users attended hands-on training sessions to learn the new e-file software. They then received support from local champions and their line managers, and training manuals and videos were put on the intranet. Targets were unofficially relaxed for a while to give people the time to learn and try out new things.
Change brings more work: Unfortunately, this is usually true. Planning and implementing change requires extra effort from people who are usually already fully utilised with 'business as usual' work.	Release people to work on the change where possible. Plan change in less busy business as usual times. Put change objectives in personal development plans to make sure people are rewarded for their extra effort. Say thank you and celebrate major milestones.	**Mayer & Co E-file:** Change champions who were heavily involved in testing the new e-file software had temporary staff brought in to undertake their business as usual roles. Their champion roles were also written into their personal objectives to make sure their contribution and new skills were recorded and rewarded appropriately. After each phase of the implementation, a lunch was held for the relevant champions to say thank you for all their hard work.
Ripple effects: Change disturbs the activities of lots of stakeholders, not just those immediately affected. Those affected at 'arm's length' may experience disruption without any apparent benefit from the change.	Make sure you have identified everyone who is affected by the change. Work with them to keep them informed and engaged and to minimise disruption. Identify any benefits they may realise or enable due to the change.	**Spark Clearholme Office Move:** One department was not moving, as their teams were to be disbanded before the current lease ran out. Work was done with them to make sure they could deal with the practical effects of the change, for example that they knew how to book meeting rooms in the new building, and to make sure they did not feel left out and demotivated, for example by keeping the gym and canteen open in the old office block for them.

(Continued)

Table 5.1 (Continued)

Reason for Resistance	Preventions	Example
Past resentments surface: Organisations are built on complex and sometimes fragile personal relationships. Introducing change can disturb tentative steady-state relationships and reopen old wounds, causing tension, unhappiness, and resistance to the change.	Research the history of the organisation and try to identify where fragile relationships exist. Try to heal old wounds where possible before launching into your change. Try to build incentives and motivations into your change solution which will help to minimise the effects of opening old wounds.	**Mayer & Co E-file:** Two support departments, the post room and general administration, were significantly affected by the implementation of e-file. Both the department heads had worked at Mayer for a number of years. Early on in their working relationship, they developed a mutual dislike for each other which neither could overcome. They had settled into a fragile truce where they had as little as possible to do with each other and designed their teams to work as independently of each other as possible. The two heads were unable to work constructively together to find a positive solution to the e-file change. External facilitation was needed to help them discuss and reach sensible conclusions about the best future for the organisation and their teams, putting personal emotions aside.
Sometimes the threat is real: Change can hurt. On a personal level, it can result in a loss of jobs, power, responsibility, money, status, or career prospects. On an organisational level, it can result in more work, less efficient ways of doing things, greater risk and pressure, and less resource.	Try to design the change to minimise negative effects where possible. Be honest and transparent about what is changing and why. Be quick where possible, for example don't let uncertainty about job security linger any longer than it has to. Offer support to people who are hurt by the change.	**Workout! Restructure:** The restructure meant that three volunteer roles were to be amalgamated into one paid role in each new area. A fair, transparent recruitment process was held and the decision on who to employ was made the same day as the interviews to minimise waiting time for the candidates. The unsuccessful candidates were informed by phone rather than by letter or email and given honest feedback on why they did not meet the criteria for the role, to keep the process as objective and dignified as possible.

It is important to engage with vocal resistors to try and find out what they are really concerned about. Make sure you do this on a one-to-one basis to prevent exaggerated behaviours in front of an audience. Sometimes vocal resistors are not keen to explain the real reason they are worried – perhaps they think the change will show them up as having a weakness or they risk some less-than-best practice being unearthed. In these cases, they often pick another issue to object to or complain about everything to do with the change to hide the real problem. It may also be possible that they have a specific concern which is highly relevant and which, if dealt with, could significantly improve either the change itself or your change approach. It is easy to class vocal resistors as troublemakers and try to suppress or ignore them. But doing this risks missing the chance to collect valuable information and make improvements to your change.

Box 5.1 Vocal resistance to Burntwood's EDRMS

Ever since the idea of implementing an EDRMS was mentioned in Burntwood, the Head of Adult Services had been unhappy. He spoke to his line manager, the programme sponsor, the programme team, his operational team, his colleagues, and even the Chief Executive Officer about what a mistake an EDRMS would be for Burntwood. He believed that no-one would like it, it would not solve any problems but create lots more, it would be so difficult to use that everyone would avoid it, and the change would be an unmitigated disaster. He brought up the subject in one-to-one discussions, team meetings, workshops, and even when passing programme team members in the corridor! He had a reputation as being quite a difficult character so his objections were largely ignored and his involvement in the programme was minimised. However, his constant complaining was beginning to affect his colleagues and team members, who were losing confidence in the change and starting to question how successful an EDRMS would be.

The business change manager invited the Head of Adult Services for an informal chat over coffee and explained that she was keen to understand his objections as he may have valuable information which would help Burntwood increase the success of the change. Given the opportunity to talk calmly and fully, the Head explained that he had experienced an EDRMS implementation in his previous place of work. He had since heard from ex-colleagues that it had proved very unpopular – adoption was minimal, quality of work had been affected, and morale had plummeted. He was passionate about Burntwood County Council, really believing they made a positive difference to their service users, and did not want to see the same failure happen there.

Once these worries had surfaced, the business change manager organised a visit to the Head's previous organisation to meet his successor. She saw how users were expected to use the EDRMS and was shown the areas which were cumbersome and unpopular and which were causing all the problems. It transpired that these problems were due to poor design choices which could be rectified in the Burntwood EDRMS, resulting in a simpler and more acceptable system. The Head of Adult Services was kept informed of the findings and invited to an early demonstration of Burntwood's EDRMS to see where the relevant changes had been made. Whilst he never fully got over his distrust of the system, he accepted that the main issues had been rectified and reduced his resistance to the change.

People being very quiet and disengaging from the change, including

- Agreeing to proposals without questioning them;
- Not turning up to presentations, meetings, and workshops;
- Cancelling one-to-one appointments to discuss the change;
- Agreeing to undertake preparation activities then not doing so.

As this resistant behaviour manifests itself through avoidance, it is very easy to miss, especially if you are having to deal with lots of vocal resistors or there are other urgent and important issues vying for your attention.

A key risk of failing to recognise this type of resistance is that you miss vital information and ideas during the planning of your change. Not only will your change be the poorer for these omissions, but also disengaged resistors then have the potential to raise essential issues at the last minute and derail implementation. In addition, disengaged managers give out a very powerful message to their teams, minimising the chance of any successful changes in their areas.

People may be disengaged for a number of reasons, including lack of time, unhappiness with aspects of the change, denial, cynicism that the change will happen, or because their motivations are driving them in a different direction. Keep your eyes open for any hint of disengagement amongst your stakeholders and be very careful if you run a presentation, meeting, or workshop about your change and there are no questions or opposition – this does not mean that you have been successful in getting your stakeholders on board, more probably that you have failed to engage at all!

Box 5.2   A disengaged branch of Workout!

During the planning of the Workout! restructure, it became apparent that the Scottish branch was very disengaged with the change. No representatives had been involved in the planning workshops, and no Scottish members had fed back any thoughts, questions, or issues during a very active consultation exercise. All other branches had been involved in the two activities, making the disengagement obvious through comparison.

In order to overcome the resistance, the London-based change team tried to arrange a trip to Scotland to discuss the change face to face with their Scottish colleagues. The branch agreed in principle but failed to find a suitable time and venue, resulting in the meeting being delayed indefinitely. Eventually, the change team decided to travel up to Scotland on the day that the Scottish branch was holding its annual meeting. They asked the CEO to organise a slot on the agenda for them and booked their plane tickets. Under these circumstances, it was difficult for the branch to find a suitable excuse, so the engagement finally went ahead.

During the meeting, the change team explained the drivers for the change and why Workout! could not continue to operate in the old ways. They highlighted the expected benefits for Workout!'s customers in Scotland, which raised some interest from the branch members who were passionate about supporting their customers in the best ways they could. The change team then asked the branch if they would pilot one of the changes which would be of most benefit to their customers. The branch was very interested in this idea and started asking questions about how it would work and discussing how best to approach it. The disengagement was over.

People actively work against the change to sabotage it, including

- Spreading negative stories and rumours about the change;
- Upsetting meetings and workshops by raising irrelevant issues and refusing to move on from them;
- Refusing to follow new ways of working in order to make the change fail.

Sabotage is mainly subversive, so it is difficult to identify this type of resistance before damage is done. Some sabotage is very sophisticated – it is not unusual for saboteurs to put far more effort into resisting than they would ever need to make the change. This is a timely reminder of how deeply change can affect people.

One of the main problems with this type of resistance is that new products, processes, and behaviours are very fragile in their early stages and easily disrupted and broken. If someone puts their mind to upsetting your change through sabotage, they will probably succeed. People's confidence in change is equally fragile in the early days, and rumours and stories of things going wrong will quickly escalate and significantly reduce support for your change. Therefore, it pays to be vigilant throughout all stages of the change journey and investigate every story and rumour you hear for infiltration by saboteurs. All that said, providing sabotage does not seriously damage your change it can be rather entertaining in hindsight. One of my favourite sabotage stories is described in Box 5.3.

Box 5.3   Real-life example: sabotaging an office move

A large, established insurance company moved offices as part of a wider cultural change to bring siloed departments together to work more closely. As part of the move, hotdesking was introduced to encourage collaboration and break down traditional hierarchies. All seemed to go smoothly until a few days after the move when the change manager became aware of an emerging issue. Every morning, the technology support desk was receiving a number of calls from staff reporting that the computers at certain desks were not working. However, when engineers called at the desks to investigate, there was nothing wrong and the computers were working perfectly.

Stories were beginning to spread amongst the staff that there was something wrong with the technology in the new offices. Confidence was being undermined and support for the new hotdesking policy was diminishing rapidly, with users keen to settle at desks where they were certain the computers worked.

The change manager decided to investigate. He stayed late after work that night and observed a small group of users visiting a number of computers after everyone else had left the office, pocketing a small but vital 'dongle' from each one. Without this dongle, the computers would not work.

The next morning the rest of the staff arrived at the office and chose a hot desk to sit at. A number of these staff soon realised that the computers at their desks were not working. They reported the faults to the technology support desk, complained to their colleagues about the waste of time, and moved desks. The saboteurs then arrived at the affected desks, inserted the dongles back into the computers and settled down to work. By the time the engineers arrived to investigate, nothing was wrong.

With a bit of detective work, the root of the problem had been discovered and all that was left was to decide how best to deal with the saboteurs. Whilst the change manager could have officially reported them, resulting in a public and humiliating disciplinary process, he recognised that their actions had resulted from the pressure they had felt from the change and decided to manage it more informally. He had an unofficial chat with the group which was enough to make them realise the potential consequences of their behaviour and give them a chance to air their feelings about the change. After this chat, the change manager kept an eye on the group for the next few weeks but there were no more problems and the temporary technical failures soon faded from memory.

What happens next?

- Analyse your change and change approach to see whether any of the common causes of resistance are apparent. If so, either try to eliminate them through amending your change or change approach or prepare for possible resistance through building appropriate interventions into your change plan. More information on developing the change plan is given in Chapter 6.

• Prepare yourself and your change colleagues to watch out for resistant behaviour. Deal with any resistance quickly and respectfully before it causes any damage to your change and remember that resistance is usually a good indicator that your change could be done better!

References and further reading

Busby, N. 2014. Change Readiness, Planning and Measurement. In Smith, R., King, D., Sidhu, R. and Skelsey, D., eds. *The Effective Change Manager's Handbook*. London: Kogan Page, pp. 290–328

Cameron, E. and Green, M. 2009. *Making Sense of Change Management*. 2nd ed. London: Kogan Page

Kotter, John P. 1995. Leading Change: Why Transformation Efforts Fail. *Harvard Business Review*, [online]. Available at: <https://hbr.org/1995/05/leading-change-why-transformation-efforts-fail-2> [Accessed 12 January 2017]

Moss Kanter, R. 2012. Ten Reasons Why People Resist Change. *Harvard Business Review*, [online]. Available at: <https://hbr.org/2012/09/ten-reasons-people-resist-chang> [Accessed 12 January 2017]

6   Shaping your change plan

Now you have completed your initial analysis about your specific and unique change situation, it is time to bring all of this information together and plan the interventions needed to engage your stakeholders, build support for your change, and ensure everyone affected is willing and able to change their ways of working to successfully transition into the new world.

These interventions are normally pulled together into a change plan. Due to the huge variety of organisational cultures, types of changes, and attitudes and concerns of stakeholders, every change plan will vary in the amount and types of interventions needed. Chapters 7, 8, and 9 explore some common change interventions which you may want to put in your change plan, including:

- **Engaging individuals**, including senior leaders, middle managers, and staff and developing a change champion network;
- **Building support** by involving users in designing the change, running demonstrations, and creating small changes and quick wins;
- **Communications**, including organisation-wide communications and tailored communications;
- **Learning and training**, including classroom-based training, e-learning, written instructions, super users and floorwalkers, and one-to-one support.

It is important to realise that however carefully you plan your interventions at the start of your change there will always need to be a degree of flexibility as the change journey progresses, depending on the actions and reactions from your stakeholders. Make sure your change leaders are aware of this and familiarise yourself with how easy or otherwise it will be to amend, add, or omit planned activities as you go along.

What does a change management plan look like?

There is no set way to put together a change management plan. As it is just a mechanism for organising and recording your change interventions, it should be put together in a way that is readable and acceptable to your decision makers. If your organisation likes diagrams, create a diagram; if your organisation is familiar with spreadsheets, organise your plan within a spreadsheet. Using familiar formats will ease the process of getting feedback and sign-off for your plan and increase your change leaders' confidence in your abilities. This may seem a small point, but sometimes the smallest gestures can make a big difference in the world of organisational change.

Your change plan, at a minimum, should include the following information:

• What the change intervention is
• What the intervention aims to do
• Which stakeholders are targeted by the intervention
• How you will know the intervention worked.

We often refer to taking users through a 'journey' during change initiatives. Therefore, it can be helpful to shape your change plan to reflect this approach. AIDA is a popular and simple framework, originating from the world of marketing, which can be used in your change plan to illustrate how your interventions support this user journey. The four AIDA steps are:

A = **Attention:** People become aware that the change is happening and why;
I = **Interest:** People engage with the change and understand that it will affect them and the way they work;
D = **Desire:** People buy into the change, understand how it will benefit them, and actively look forward to changing;
A = **Action:** People know what they need to do differently in order to change and then make the decision to change.

Box 6.1 and Table 6.1 show excerpts from the change management plans for Burntwood EDRMS and Spark Clearholme's office move. Notice that they are in different formats, reflecting the preferred approaches of the two organisations, and that Spark Clearholme's plan uses the AIDA framework. The complete change management plan for Burntwood can be found in Appendix B.

Box 6.1   Excerpt from the change management plan for Burntwood EDRMS

Change activity 1: engaging leaders and making the case for change

Issue: major risk of resistance to new ways of working from all levels of the organisation.

   Activity: face-to-face meetings with all senior leaders across organisation (approximately sixty):

• Inform them of aims of programme;
• Make the case for change by emphasising the drivers for change;
• Find out questions, issues, and suggested improvements from leaders based on the knowledge of their teams and culture of the organisation;

- Outline next steps and gain their commitment to actively supporting the programme.

Desired outcome: increased buy-in and decreased resistance from the top of the organisation.

Measurement: After meeting, senior leaders feel positive about the change and actively lead their teams through the transition, giving staff time to engage with the programme and encouraging them through the challenges of transition.

Change activity 2: involving users at a local level – creating a change champion network

Issue: Changes to behaviour and culture need to happen at a very local level within the organisation, involving 150 teams and 1,800 individuals.

Activity: Set up EDRMS champion network – sixty users based in the business who can communicate programme messages to their colleagues and feedback issues, suggestions, and problems to the programme.

Desired outcome: Local intelligence gathered from the champions will enable the programme to tailor support and interventions depending on the impact of the change on teams, the level of enthusiasm or resistance to the change, and the influential capacity of individuals within the team.

Measurement: Champions in each local area gathering feedback. Teams engaged and bought into the change through tailored support and intervention from individual champions.

Table 6.1 Excerpt from the change management plan for Spark Clearholme's office move

AIDA Stage	Initiative	Objective	Practicalities	Measurement
Attention	Set up relocation group – representatives who will lead on the change in their area	One representative from each local area who will give out information, feedback issues and questions, and make sure move activities are carried out in their area	Meet once a month – more frequently once move commences	Reps recruited for all areas and actively engaging with the group and their colleagues
Interest	Intranet pages for all staff	Provide an intranet site as a one-stop shop for regular quick updates, including: • Floor plans • Photos • Move schedule • Answers to questions raised by relocation group	In place before organisation-wide announcement goes out and then update weekly	Number of hits on the intranet pages Number and type of questions asked by staff to the relocation group and project team

How many change interventions do you need?

Not all change requires the same number or type of change interventions. There is no use in 'using a sledge hammer to crack a nut' and developing a very resource intensive, elaborate change plan if it is not needed. Conversely, and more usually, it is dangerous to underestimate the amount of change interventions needed, resulting in low buy-in, high resistance, and users failing to transition to new ways of thinking, behaving, and working.

The information you have gathered in preparation for developing the change plan will help you to decide how intensive your change approach should be. As a general rule, the number and intensity of your change management interventions will increase depending on the following factors:

- The bigger the impact of the change on people, especially changes to organisational culture and individual behaviours;
- The greater the number and diversity of the stakeholders affected, and the more significant their attitudes and concerns towards the change;
- The less mature and confident the organisation is in managing change, and the number of other changes the organisation is experiencing at the same time;
- The more constraints there are around how the change is planned and implemented.

Appendix B outlines the change plan for Burntwood's EDRMS programme. The change interventions are quite numerous and complex due to the large impact on culture and behaviours, the wide diversity of stakeholders, and the minimal levels of confidence and maturity Burntwood has in managing change.

You may find, having created your change management plan, that you need extra resources to successfully execute the interventions. Every intervention will require time and effort to prepare and run, so you may need more staff to help you. You may need financial resources for materials and venues or specific expertise such as trainers and facilitators. Offering refreshments is a fail-safe way of getting people to attend meetings, workshops, and training sessions, so resources will also be required for these.

Be prepared to fight hard for extra resources for change. Most organisations are understandably reluctant to spend money unless absolutely necessary, so you will need to make a compelling case for your request. Try to be imaginative in how you acquire resources and investigate what support you can leverage from within your organisation. For example can Learning and Development provide trainers and Internal Communications draft your organisation-wide messages? Could your change sponsor's personal assistant undertake some of your administrative tasks? Is there a budding change specialist who can be seconded onto your project as a development opportunity?

If the organisation fails to equip you with enough resources to carry out your change plan, inform your change sponsor immediately. They have a vested interest in making the change a success so should be able to rectify the issue. If the resources are still not forthcoming and your sponsor is fully aware of the implications of under-resourcing the change, you need to think hard about your continued involvement. Organisational change is tough, and failure levels are high. Change managers are not miracle workers, and change can be successful only if it has adequate support and resources – don't let yourself get involved in a change which is set up to fail.

Box 6.2   Resources needed for Burntwood's EDRMS change plan

The Burntwood EDRMS change plan required the services of a full-time business change manager, three full-time user support officers (see Chapter 7 for more information about these roles), two full-time trainers, one full-time communications officer, one part time administrator and sixty volunteer change champions.

Enough finance was required for a specialist facilitator, venue, materials, and refreshments for the champion induction day; materials and printing for training manuals and awareness posters; materials and refreshments for workshops and meetings; and funding for a thank you party for all key stakeholders and users after the implementation was completed. One of the organisation's dedicated training rooms was hired out for a year to hold change interventions such as workshops, demonstrations, and classroom-based training.

Integrating change plans and implementation plans

Alongside the development of your change plan, there will need to be a plan developed to implement the practical things needed for the change to happen. In a project environment, this will be done by the project manager. If your change is not being run as a project, it may be the responsibility of a local manager, appointed change lead, or subject matter expert. Depending on the circumstances, it may even be yourself.

Make sure that you work closely with whoever is developing the implementation or project plan to ensure you are working to the same timescales and that vital activities are not duplicated across the plans or missing completely.

It will probably be the implementation plan that your change leaders are most interested in monitoring throughout the change journey. Therefore, make sure your key change activities and their timings are added to this plan – you will then be able to report on how they are going and have more support if needed to solve problems or deal with issues.

Typical change activities and milestones you may want to add to an implementation plan include:

- Setting up a champion network
- Dates for key stakeholder meetings and demonstrations

- Dates for key communications to users about the change
- Dates for training sessions
- Floorwalking support after implementation.

Just like change management plans, implementation plans can alter a lot throughout the change journey. Therefore, you need to keep in very close contact with whoever is managing the implementation of the change to make sure that any alterations to their plan are reflected in the timings and content of your change interventions and vice versa. The plans may need to be updated more than once before the delivery of the change is complete.

Box 6.3   Interdependence between change and implementation at Spark Clearholme

During the marketing campaign planning change at Spark Clearholme, a project manager was responsible for implementing the campaign planning technology and a change manager was responsible for ensuring all users would buy into and use the tool once implemented.

After initial engagement with the affected team leaders by the change manager, the project manager developed an implementation plan which would enable enough time for the technology to be built and tested fully. The change manager then drafted her change plan to ensure all stakeholders would be trained and fully prepared to start using the tool by the implementation dates. However, when the team leaders saw the number of training and preparation activities needed, they asked the change manager to postpone the activities by four weeks to a time when the teams would have less business as usual work to do and could concentrate fully on the change. The change manager amended her plan and then passed it to the project manager to update the implementation plan accordingly.

Shortly after the plans were agreed, the project manager had to delay the implementation of the software by another month due to problems with early testing. Before the new implementation dates could be planned, the change manager had to consult the team leaders to check that the teams would still have time to focus on the change in one month's time. Once this was confirmed, both plans were updated to reflect the new delivery dates.

Potential tensions between change and implementation

There is an inherent conflict between business change and project delivery. The project or implementation manager's aim is to prepare and introduce tangible changes into the organisation, whereas the business change manager's aim is to ensure everyone accepts the change and adjusts their ways of working, thinking, and behaving to realise the benefits.

As the majority of change initiatives has limitations on resources, time, and access to users, there is often tension between these two sets of aims. The amount of time needed to prepare the tangible changes and prepare the users to accept them can vary enormously, and with limited resources and access to users, there are often compromises to be made between the business change and project activities.

This tension is often felt at the end of a project, when the physical changes may have been implemented successfully, but the users have not yet truly adopted and embedded them. More information about this is given in Chapter 11. You may also experience this tension much earlier in your change initiative, especially in organisations where budgets and resources are in short supply and the emphasis is on rolling out change as quickly as possible to reduce project costs and realise financial benefits. In these cases, implementation timelines are often dictated by how long it will take to prepare and introduce the physical change without much consideration being given to how long it may take to ensure users are ready to successfully adopt it.

If you find yourself in this situation, you may find your carefully researched and tailored change management approach is threatened. If this happens, here are a few ideas of how to engage and persuade your key decision makers that the need for focussed business change is necessary for the benefits of the change to be realised:

- Undertake an impact assessment to illustrate how much higher the impact of the change will be without your proposed change interventions.
- List the risks to the success of the change initiative if the change interventions do not take place, including increased resistance, lack of adoption, and subsequent failure to realise the expected benefits. If you have a risk register for the change initiative, enter these as red (urgent) risks. If you don't have a formal risk register, ensure all your key decision makers are made explicitly aware of the risks and how change management interventions could mitigate them.
- Calculate the cost of not realising the benefits of the change and compare it with the cost of your proposed change initiatives. Remember that costs go way beyond not realising financial benefits, including risk to the quality of business as usual work during the change and loss of goodwill, trust, and cooperation in any future changes the organisation may have planned.
- Ask influential and supportive users to petition key decision makers. Decision makers are far more likely to listen to and appreciate issues when they are communicated from within affected user communities than from a business change manager.

Box 6.4 Deciding how to implement Burntwood's EDRMS

Like many technology changes, it was perfectly possible for all 1,800 users across Burntwood County Council to go live with the EDRMS software at the same time. Therefore, by default, any other implementation approach had additional time, cost, and resource implications.

The business change manager did not feel that a 'big bang' implementation would be successful for users, as it would allow very limited time for engagement and user support. Therefore, she prepared a report for the change sponsor and other key decision makers outlining the risks of this approach, including:

- The size and types of impact the change would have on Burntwood, especially the need for major cultural and behavioural change amongst users;
- The fact that Burntwood's core activities would be seriously affected by a failure of the EDRMS;
- The overall lack of enthusiasm for the change, and potential areas of resistance within Burntwood;
- The organisation's less-than-successful history with managing change.

From this report, the key decision makers realised that in order for the benefits to be realised from the EDRMS change, a slower implementation was needed in order to engage with and support users during the change. Therefore, it was decided to implement the system in phases to make sure that all teams were supported properly. Even though this meant that the implementation took months rather than days, the approach resulted in high adoption rates and successful benefits realisation, which more than compensated for the increased length of time for implementation.

How to measure the effectiveness of your change interventions

For anyone who has read this far into the book, it will come as no surprise to learn that there is no simple, straightforward way to measure the impact of your change activities. Reactions to change consist of complex patterns of behaviour and internal processes which are different for each individual and not directly observable. The decision each individual takes to either engage in or resist the change is based on a combination of opinions, attitudes, motivation, emotions, reactions, behaviours, and personalities, as well as a myriad of outside influences. Therefore, isolating and measuring the impact of your change activities on an individual's intention to change can be challenging.

These challenges do not mean that measuring the impact of change management interventions cannot be done with a fair degree of accuracy. However, measurement itself is an activity which takes up time, resources, and the goodwill of your users. You need to strike a balance between taking enough measurement to confirm that your change interventions are making a positive impact and the effort and resources needed to take the measurement.

Business change is successful only if it assists users through their change journey to eventual adoption and embedding of the change. Therefore, the success of your interventions can be measured only by the cumulative pattern of user movement through that journey, rather than by the success of individual interventions. This is illustrated in Figure 6.1. Make sure you choose measurements that really illustrate how your interventions are making an impact. For example measuring the number of users who attend a demonstration of your change will not give a clear indication of how the demonstration has impacted how your users feel about the change. Measuring how enthusiastic users feel about the change before and after the demonstration, however, will indicate whether the intervention has increased support for the change, and therefore whether it will help users along their journey to eventual adoption and embedding.

Figure 6.1 shows the measurements taken by the change manager for Burntwood's EDRMS initiative to show if her interventions were guiding users successfully along their change journey. The change intervention numbers at the top of the diagram correspond with the associated change management activities in the Burntwood change plan outlined in Appendix B. Note that this diagram measures up to implementation only. Measurements for embedding and sustainability once the change has been implemented are covered in Chapter 11.

You will notice that a range of measurement techniques are used for the EDRMS change interventions. Three of the most common techniques used for measuring the impact of change interventions are explored in the following sections.

Pulse surveys

Quick, one-off question tallies used to gauge opinion on a specific subject with a yes or no answer. The survey can be carried out in a number of ways, for example by placing voting tokens and boxes in reception areas, putting flip chart tally sheets on the wall, or placing voting buttons on intranet sites.

Pulse surveys are useful for taking a quick temperature check about the change and can be repeated at intervals to measure progress. They are quick for users to participate in and can be fun, so you should get a good response. Make sure your question fits neatly into a yes or no answer. For example a pulse survey can be used to ask if people have heard about your change but not to ascertain what they have heard or how they feel about it.

In-depth surveys

These are a series of questions usually sent out electronically through specialist software such as SurveyMonkey. They are good for taking a snapshot of opinions and feelings at a moment in time from a large group of people so can be used to benchmark how people feel about your change. They can then be repeated after a number of change interventions have taken place to measure whether opinions and feelings have increased in positivity.

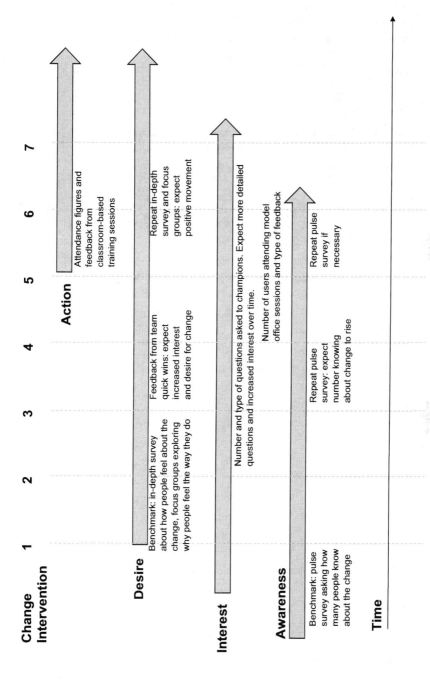

Change Intervention

1   2   3   4   5   6   7

Action

Desire

Benchmark: in-depth survey about how people feel about the change, focus groups exploring why people feel the way they do

Feedback from team quick wins: expect increased interest and desire for change

Repeat in-depth survey and focus groups: expect positive movement

Attendance figures and feedback from classroom-based training sessions

Interest

Number and type of questions asked to champions. Expect more detailed questions and increased interest over time.

Awareness

Number of users attending model office sessions and type of feedback

Benchmark: pulse survey asking how many people know about the change

Repeat pulse survey: expect number knowing about change to rise

Repeat pulse survey if necessary

Time

Figure 6.1 Success measures for Burntwood's EDRMS change interventions

Make sure your survey is quick and easy to fill in to encourage users to participate – seven to ten questions is usually ample. Beware of asking leading questions, those which encourage the answer you desire, and always test the survey in advance with a small group to ensure that the questions are clear and unambiguous. Surveys will tell you what people think and feel but not why, so they are often accompanied by focus groups to explore the answers in more depth.

Focus groups

These are face-to-face workshops with small groups of users (between five and ten people), where you can explore the reasons behind thoughts, feelings, and opinions in significant depth. Groups usually last about one hour, and asking lots of open questions – those requiring more thought and more explanation than a simple yes or no answer – can encourage attendees to explore the root causes of why they feel or behave as they do towards aspects of your change.

Try to hold a number of focus groups with a range of users to get a wide picture of thoughts and concerns. If you are repeating your focus group throughout your change journey to measure progress, try to invite the same attendees to all repeat sessions to maintain continuity and make your measurements more robust.

References and further reading

Busby, N. 2014. Change Readiness, Planning and Measurement. In Smith, R., King, D., Sidhu, R. and Skelsey, D., eds. *The Effective Change Manager's Handbook*. London: Kogan Page, pp. 290–328

Dibb, S., Simkin, L., Pride, W. and Ferrell, O. 2006. *Marketing Concepts and Strategies*. 5th ed. Abingdon: Houghton Mifflin

Price, P. 2012. *Research Methods in Psychology: Core Concepts and Skills*. Washington: Flat World Knowledge

Sidhu, R. 2014. Communications and Engagement. In Smith, R., King, D., Sidhu, R. and Skelsey, D., eds. *The Effective Change Manager's Handbook*. London: Kogan Page, pp. 210–257

Part two

Common change interventions

7 Engaging individuals and building support

The importance of engaging individuals

A key theme of this book is that the benefits of organisational change will be realised only if every affected individual decides to make the effort to change the way they work and behave. Some level of engagement is needed for every individual in order for that to happen. These engagement interventions will vary depending on the roles and responsibilities of the individuals during the change, which fall into three broad categories:

1 Senior leaders who make key decisions and own and resource the change;
2 Middle managers who lead and support their staff through the change;
3 Staff, or end users, who each need to decide to make the change.

Engaging senior leaders

You must have senior leader support for your change initiative; otherwise, the chances of success are very slim. One senior leader with weight, respect, and gravitas amongst their peers needs to take on the responsibility of championing and sponsoring the change from the initial idea to embedding and benefits realisation. In addition, your change needs to be supported by the majority, ideally all, of the other affected senior leaders. Any leaders who actively oppose your change should be seen as a significant threat. You need to weigh up their power against the power of the leaders who actively support your change and make sure the balance of power is, and remains, in your favour. More information about how to analyse and manage key stakeholders can be found in Chapter 4: Understanding Stakeholder Engagement.

Given their seniority, limited availability, and access to sensitive information, senior leaders are best engaged on a one-to-one basis. You need to decide who is the best person to engage with each leader – it may not necessarily be you, especially if you are working as an external consultant or short-term contractor. Senior leaders may prefer to engage with someone who works full time for their organisation, whom they know (by name if not personally), and whom they trust to do the best for the organisation and the people within it. Find out who each leader respects and listens to and whose opinion they value. This may be one of your change team or champions or even your change sponsor or another of their senior leader colleagues.

Box 7.1   Engaging senior leaders in the Burntwood EDRMS programme

At the beginning of the EDRMS programme, sixty senior leaders across Burntwood were identified as being affected by the change. Each one was invited to a one-to-one meeting to introduce them to the programme, explain the benefits of the EDRMS and the risks it was mitigating, and give them a brief outline of timescales and what the change involved. They were encouraged to ask questions about the change, raise any issues or concerns, and offer any suggestions or thoughts.

The programme's director, the programme manager, and the business change manager allocated the meetings out between them, on the basis of any knowledge or previous working relationships with the senior leaders or who was most appropriate in terms of background, personality, and job role. The two exceptions to this were the CEO and the IT Director who, due to availability, seniority, and personality, were met by the programme sponsor. A brief outline of what was to be covered in each meeting was agreed so the same information was imparted to everyone, and results of the meetings were shared regularly between the three managers and the sponsor.

Each meeting lasted up to thirty minutes and the initiative took a total of six weeks to complete. The initiative was resource intensive but provided a huge amount of valuable information for the programme, including which senior leaders were supportive, who was not so keen, and who was actively hostile. Information was also obtained about which areas of the change interested or concerned each stakeholder and many thoughts and suggestions were gathered. Personalised engagement activities were then developed for each senior leader over the course of the programme to maintain support from the enthusiasts and to build enthusiasm from those who were not so sure.

Some practical tips for engaging senior leaders

Engaging senior leaders can be a challenge – they are very busy, their diaries are constantly changing as last-minute issues arise, and they may not see you or your change as a priority. It can also be daunting and difficult, especially if they are not supportive of your change. If you find yourself struggling to engage successfully with your senior leaders, here are some tips that may help:

*   Build good relationships with personal assistants and secretaries. They are enormously powerful, as they guard access to the senior leaders and can really help you with your engagement attempts.

- Be flexible and ready to drop everything if a last minute opportunity arises to speak to the senior leader.
- Be clear on what you want from the meeting – practise your summary of the change so it is short, clear, and concise. Research how the change will affect each leader in advance so you can focus on what they are interested in.
- Research how best to engage and communicate with each senior leader. People who work with them regularly will be able to give you useful tips such as whether they like to receive papers in advance, if they prefer to focus on facts and figures or wider concepts, and what their general concerns and interests are. Use this to shape your engagement approach to get the best response from each leader.
- Take a written list of items you want to cover into the meeting to ensure you don't forget anything, especially if the meeting turns out to be challenging or wanders off-topic.
- Agree with each leader how they want to be communicated with after the meeting – do they want to meet regularly or receive regular email updates, or do they only want to be contacted when they need to do something or a problem arises they need to know about?
- If either you or the leader takes away any actions, make sure you agree a date by which these will be done. Ensure you complete your actions within the agreed timeframe and chase if theirs become outstanding.
- Summarise the main points of the discussion in an email and send it to the leader as a record of the meeting. This is especially important if they made a decision in the meeting, agreed to carry out any actions, or asked you to do something for them.
- If you can't access senior leaders on a one-to-one basis, try to organise a presentation about your change initiative at an executive or leadership meeting. You can then follow up personally with any leaders who have questions or ask a friendly stakeholder who is close to the individual leaders to check with them whether more engagement is needed.

Supporting middle managers

Middle managers (those who manage the teams of people on the 'front line' of the organisation) are another powerful group during organisational change. They are often collectively known as 'corporate glue' – the people who hold the organisation together by translating ideas from the top of the organisation into actions at the bottom. Teams look to their managers to lead them in action, behaviour, and attitude, so engaged and enthusiastic middle managers can really help the success of your change.

If your organisation is mature in implementing change, you should find that the middle managers are expecting to work in partnership with you to successfully implement your change in their areas. In mature organisations, change works best when middle managers are given responsibility for their teams implementing and adopting the change and you provide them with enough information and support for them to do this.

It is vital that you work closely with this group during your change. The quickest way to disempower middle managers is to engage their staff without letting them know what is going on. Don't forget – middle managers are responsible for maintaining good business as usual activities as well as implementing the change and are also the ones their staff will look to for guidance and go to with any questions and issues. Keep them informed and provide them with enough information about the change that they can manage their team's time effectively and deal with any questions and issues.

Box 7.2   Implementing e-file through middle managers at Mayer & Co

Legal caseworkers at Mayer & Co were divided into departments, each led by two department heads who split ten teams between them, each led by a team manager.

In order to plan how to implement to each department, the business change manager met with the department heads and together they decided on the following implementation activities for each department.

Team manager briefings: Led by the relevant heads and supported by the business change manager, each department held a briefing for the team managers to discuss the details, benefits, and impacts of the change and the role expected of the team managers. The heads followed this up with individual meetings to make sure the managers were comfortable with their role and had enough support to carry it out successfully.

Departmental emails: Two emails were sent out to the departments at key points during the change. The first was at the beginning of the preparation period to let the department know that e-file was coming and outlining the preparation and engagement activities needed. The second was sent just before implementation to let them know the key dates and what would happen during implementation. In both cases, the emails were drafted by the business change manager, who knew all the details, finalised and signed by the department heads, and sent out by the team managers. This sent a clear message to all staff that every layer of management was supportive of e-file and that making the change successful was the responsibility of everyone within the department.

Demonstrations: Each team, accompanied by its team manager, attended a demonstration of the e-file system to see what an electronic case file looked like and to look at some of the key features of the system. This gave each team a chance to discuss how they would make e-file work in their area and gave the team managers an opportunity to assess how big a change it would be for their staff and which staff may need more support during implementation. They could then prepare their own activities and approaches for supporting and leading their teams through the change.

Running the demonstrations was very resource intensive – four members of the project team held more than 100 one-hour sessions over the course of the implementation. However, the investment was worthwhile as the demonstrations were a key activity for getting buy-in for the change and supporting team managers to lead their staff throughout the implementation.

Potential issues with middle managers

Do not assume that all middle managers will be supportive of your change. Middle management is a tough place to sit in organisations, with a constant need to prioritise initiatives, balance change implementation with business as usual targets, and cope with needs and issues coming down from their bosses and up from their staff. You may find this is the group in the organisation who has had the worst experiences of past change initiatives and is therefore the most cynical and least enthusiastic about your change. If so, you will need to actively build support for your change amongst your middle management stakeholder group before you can progress very far.

If focussed engagement interventions fail to increase support from the majority of your middle managers then, exactly as if the majority of your senior leaders is against the change, the potential for success is greatly reduced. Flag this as soon as possible with your change sponsor and other key decision makers so they are able to discuss and decide how best to proceed.

If your organisation is not mature in managing change, or middle managers are new or inexperienced, they may struggle with their responsibilities during the change. If so, your change plan will need to include training and support for middle managers on how to support their teams through change, and they will require increased support from their leaders to help them develop the essential skills and behaviours they will need. If your organisation is not keen on investing in this, or support is not forthcoming from struggling leaders, you will need to resource extra support from elsewhere to help managers and teams with preparation and implementation activities. This can be done through either increasing the scope and support of your change champion network (more information on champions can be found later in the chapter) or providing extra resources from your change team.

Box 7.3   User support officers at Burntwood

Burntwood County Council did not have a history of managing change well, and the majority of middle managers was neither capable nor willing to actively engage with the implementation of the EDRMS. This, coupled with a lack of interest in developing the change capability of the organisation from a number of its senior leaders, meant that there was no certainty that middle managers would take responsibility for the local success of the changes. To fill this gap and offer extra support to the middle managers and their staff, four full-time User Support Officer roles were created within the EDRMS change team.

The sole responsibility of the User Support Officers was to work closely with designated teams and their managers to ensure success of the change at the local level. The officers were all seconded from different departments within Burntwood so they were known and trusted by the managers and staff and were able to work closely with the teams to support them in the vital preparation, implementation, and embedding activities needed to make the change a success.

Working with end users

Change will be truly successful and sustainable only if each affected individual, or end user, decides to make the effort to change to the new ways of working and then sticks to it. In order for this to happen, each individual will need differing levels and types of engagement, information, and support. If your change affects only a small number of people, you may be able to get to know and work with all your end users, but usually too many people are affected for this to be possible. In this case, creating a change champion network is a good way of widening your sphere of influence and offering tailored support to every individual affected by the change, no matter how large your change may be.

Creating a change champion network

Change champions are business as usual staff who either volunteer or are nominated by their manager to work with you on the change alongside their usual job. You will need at least one champion for each team, more if the teams are large or the change is very complex.

The change champions support their colleagues throughout the change and act as the link between you and the teams and individuals affected by the change. Even when middle managers are fully engaged and participating in the change, there is still a need for champions to undertake change-related activities which the middle managers will not have time to do.

Typical activities for a change champion network may include:

*   Giving out information about the change to their teams and colleagues, answering questions, and gathering suggestions;
*   Feeding back to you about how their colleagues are feeling about the change and what questions and issues are arising;

- Analysing how the change affects local ways of working and identifying benefits that can be realised in their areas;
- Supporting their team managers and colleagues to adapt to new ways of working and realise the benefits of the change;
- Leading on local preparation and implementation activities, keeping you informed of how they are progressing;
- Working with other champions across the organisation to look at the effects of the change and develop possible solutions across different departments;
- Developing and testing ideas, approaches, and solutions for the change;
- Developing in-depth knowledge about the change and challenging, constructively criticising, and suggesting best ways to approach the change for their particular areas;
- Becoming expert users in new processes or systems introduced during the change and supporting colleagues to adapt to these.

Box 7.4   Supporting staff through change champions at Mayer & Co

During the e-file change at Mayer & Co, each team leader nominated one team member to be a champion, resulting in a network of about 100 champions. All champions receive specialist training to become e-file super users (see Chapter 9 for more information on super users) and a number also volunteered to become e-file trainers to deliver the classroom-based training to their colleagues.

Shortly before implementation, a workshop was held for the champions in each department to help them decide how best to support their colleagues through the change. The champions identified the specific tasks they needed to undertake and allocated them out. These included:

- Team floorwalking
- Extra support for individuals who are struggling
- Daily feedback to the business change manager
- Communications out to the team.

The champions also developed engagement plans explaining how they would let their colleagues know who they were and how they could help during the change. They also decided how to disseminate information from the project team throughout implementation, how to identify problems and best practices, and how they would communicate amongst themselves. Each department developed slightly different ways of working based on local cultures and personalities. Ideas included:

- Putting up posters with photos of the champions
- Attending weekly team meetings to update colleagues

- Having a single email address for colleagues to email concerns and questions
- Meeting regularly amongst themselves to discuss challenges and how to tackle them.

During the first two weeks of implementation, the champions found that the role took up most of their time. The team managers ensured they were released from business as usual work in order to concentrate on the change. As their colleagues became more confident with e-file and initial issues were resolved, less support was needed and the role began to reduce.

Building support for your change

Actively building support and increasing buy-in for change is a key activity for any business change manager. Not all of your stakeholders will be supportive of your change, especially in the early stages when little detail is known and rumours are rife. Following are three change interventions which can be used to increase support and reduce resistance during the build up to implementation:

1   Involving users in designing the change
2   Demonstrations
3   Small changes and quick wins.

Involving users in designing the change

One of the biggest causes of unhappiness for users during organisational change is loss of control and feeling that change is being imposed upon them. This can be lessened by involving users in designing the change. By being involved in making decisions about what the future will look like and how it will be implemented, control is given back to users and they immediately have some buy-in and ownership of the change.

It is rarely practical to involve users in all the major decisions about a change initiative. For example many key decisions are made as a consequence of senior leaders setting corporate strategies and policies or because of legal or contractual constraints. However, when the change is planned in more detail, there are normally at least a few decisions that users can influence. Be very clear with users about what is within their power to shape, what is not up for negotiation, and why. This will manage expectations and help people understand and accept the decisions which need to be made without their input.

Table 7.1 shows where major decisions about the Burntwood EDRMS were made by senior leaders and where users were then able to actively influence the details. By involving users in this way, interest, buy-in, and ownership of the change was increased and resentment that major decisions affecting the day to day work of users were being made without their input was decreased.

Table 7.1 User involvement in decision making for Burntwood EDRMS

High Level Decision	Decision Made by	Details	User Involvement
To invest in a programme to tackle the issue of information management in Burntwood	Burntwood's corporate strategy	Would an EDRMS solve the information management issues?	Early on in the change, volunteer teams tried using an EDRMS and fed their experiences back to the programme board
To buy an EDRMS 'off the shelf' rather than to build a bespoke system for Burntwood	Burntwood's technology strategy	Which EDRMS should Burntwood buy?	Two user representatives sat on the procurement panel to help choose the EDRMS on behalf of their colleagues
Not to make any bespoke alterations to the EDRMS	Burntwood's technology strategy	Which choices should be made when the 'off the shelf' EDRMS offered more than one option?	Change champions decided amongst themselves which would be the best options for their teams
The EDRMS would be rolled out to teams in a phased approach over nine months	EDRMS programme board	When would the EDRMS be implemented for each individual team?	Team managers and champions were consulted on the best time for their implementation

Demonstrations

Demonstrating the tangible things that are going to change is a very powerful way of engaging stakeholders. Until people can actually visualise what is going to change, it is difficult for them to understand what impact it will have and to what extent they will have to do things differently. By giving users the opportunity to see, experience, and experiment, questions can be answered, fears and rumours can be reduced, and users can start to plan how they will work in the new world. Even if the demonstration raises or substantiates concerns, it is easier to discuss and explore solutions with something tangible to refer to than by relying on imagination and assumption.

Demonstrations can be anything from prototypes, model offices, dummy software, pictures, maps, screenshots, videos, podcasts, or role plays. Use your imagination to come up with interesting and engaging ways of demonstrating elements of your change – anything that can help people to visualise the change and begin to explore how they would work with it will help. The more innovative the demonstration, the more likely you are to capture people's attention and create the opportunity for dialogue that may lead to increased support.

Box 7.5   Using demonstrations to build support for Spark Clearholme's office move

Spark Clearholme's new office had smaller desks and much less storage space than users had been used to. In early user engagement about the change, reduced space and storage was one of the main sources of discontent.

A demonstration workstation was set up in the reception areas of the current offices so users could experience how the new desks felt and see how much storage space they would have. Most people reported that it was not as bad as they had imagined it would be.

One of the big user benefits of the move was the high quality of the new office. In the weeks leading up to the move, each team was offered a tour of the new building, visiting the floor where they would be sitting to get an idea of space and layout. The tour also included a visit to the new gym – a big benefit of the move – and ended at the new café where free coffee and cake were laid out for the teams. These tours raised excitement and desire for the new office and gave teams a positive feeling about the move. Even those concerned with the reduced individual desk space were able to see that the new offices had other benefits, including more overall space, lots of light, and very good cake!

Small changes and quick wins

Organisational change can be daunting for users and the more things that change, the more unnerving and overwhelming it can feel. Quite understandably, these negative feelings will reduce enthusiasm and support. If your change is large or complex, try introducing some small changes that will benefit users in advance of the major implementation. Minor but beneficial changes carried out successfully will build confidence and increase feelings of control. If small changes bring improvements, users will also be more interested in exploring the bigger benefits that will accompany the main implementation of your change.

Even if you cannot introduce any tangible changes in advance of your main implementation, there may be some behavioural changes which will bring immediate benefits. The example in Box 7.6 shows how support was increased for the Burntwood EDRMS programme through behavioural changes in the lead-up to the main implementation.

Box 7.6   Small behavioural changes before the Burntwood EDRMS implementation

One of the major behavioural changes needed for the EDRMS programme to be successful was for all Burntwood employees to start taking individual responsibility for managing their information. Early user engagement highlighted that not many people were keen on making the effort to do this.

To start introducing the new behaviours and demonstrate how little effort is actually needed to make a difference, each team in Burntwood was introduced to eight small behavioural changes they could make to improve their information management. These changes included moving important emails to a shared inbox to be accessed by colleagues if necessary and versioning shared documents in a consistent way to ensure everyone was working with the most up to date copies. Each of the changes required minimal effort from individuals, but when done by everyone in the team resulted in tangible benefits including saving time, reducing errors, and increasing quality of work.

Each team chose one of the small changes to try it out for six weeks. At the end of that time, many teams reported that they had seen real improvements and benefits from the small changes and were significantly more interested and enthusiastic about the bigger EDRMS implementation as a result.

References and further reading

Busby, N. 2014. Change Readiness, Planning and Measurement. In Smith, R., King, D., Sidhu, R. and Skelsey, D., eds. *The Effective Change Manager's Handbook*. London: Kogan Page, pp. 290–328

Kotter, John P. 1996. *Leading Change*. Boston: Harvard Business School Press

Rees, W. David and Porter, C. 2001. *Skills of Management*. 5th ed. London: Thomson Learning

Thaler, R. and Sunstein, C. 2009. *Nudge: Improving Decisions About Health, Wealth and Happiness*. New International Edition. London: Penguin

8 Communications

Communications are a key tool in business change and are used throughout the change life cycle to help with the following:

- **Informing people of the change:** what is changing, how it is changing, and when the change is going to happen. Who is leading the change and who will be affected.
- **Building support and reducing resistance:** why the change has to happen (the drivers for change) and the benefits expected from the change. Good news stories, case studies, and quick wins. Inspirational messages from change leaders.
- **Letting people know what they need to do differently:** instructions on what to do to prepare for the change and how to work in new ways. Where to go for help and support.
- **Getting feedback throughout the change life cycle:** gather thoughts, ideas, questions, and suggestions from stakeholders. Gather and disseminate best practice and amendments during embedding of the change.

For the purposes of this chapter, communications are an intervention for engaging with multiple stakeholders. One-to-one engagement with key stakeholders is discussed separately in Chapter 4.

Communications can be a very powerful and effective engagement initiative but are often complex and challenging to get right. Formal messages distributed throughout the organisation carry a lot of authority and can be difficult to amend once released. Messages may also be received and interpreted in ways you did not intend. If erroneous messages are given out or communications are badly received, the situation can quickly spiral out of control. Rumours spread, unhappiness builds, and resistance will increase. Therefore, all communications initiatives need careful planning and execution and constant surveillance to check that information is being received and interpreted as intended.

Creating a communications plan

Creating a formal plan will increase the success of your communication initiatives by helping you avoid the following pitfalls:

- Making sure you are communicating with everyone necessary and no-one is left out of messages.
- Keeping track of what you tell to whom and when. As change plans frequently alter, this is vital to help keep your stakeholders up to date.
- Making sure your communications are coherent and consistent in content, style, format, and distribution channel.
- Ensuring that your communications activities do not clash or conflict with any others, either from other change initiatives or business as usual.

What does a communications plan look like?

Just like the change management plan discussed in Chapter 6, there is no set way to put together a communications plan so develop it in a format which is familiar to the organisation and your stakeholders. The following information will be needed as a minimum:

Objective: what is to be achieved by the communication;
Audience: which of your stakeholder groups will receive the communication;
Message: what the communication will say;
Channel: how the communication will be sent out;
Sender: who the communication is coming from;
Sign-off: who needs to agree the communication before it is sent out;
Timing: when the communication will go out;
Measurement: how you will know the communication has been successful.

Table 8.1 shows an excerpt from the communications plan for the Workout! restructure. A discussion of each of the columns follows.

Objective: We first met AIDA in Chapter 6 as a useful framework for the change plan. AIDA can be used in a similar way for your communications plan to help build support and confidence throughout the change journey by first raising awareness, then interest and desire, and finally rallying people to action to make the change.

The Workout! communications plan shows one activity for each AIDA stage. You may need more, depending on the complexity of your change and the number of different stakeholders and stakeholder groups you need to communicate with.

Table 8.1 Communications plan for Workout's restructure (excerpt)

Objective	Audience	Message	Channel	Sender	Sign-off	Timing	Measurement
Attention	All volunteers	Changes to structure being planned Main drivers for the change Find out more at the annual conference	Article in quarterly volunteer newsletter	Project sponsor (Head of Employment Services)	CEO volunteer and coordinator	Last newsletter before annual conference	Branch managers to check that all volunteers have read and understood, and gather any questions or feedback
Interest	All volunteers	Outline of new structure Reiterate main drivers and benefits Outline next steps	Presentation at the annual conference	CEO	Project sponsor and volunteer coordinator	At annual conference	Attendee survey after conference
Desire	Volunteer teams in local branches	What is changing at a local level Benefits for branches and customers Any questions and feedback	Meetings with local branches	Change manager	Project sponsor and volunteer coordinator	Two months before implementation	Number of attendees; types of questions and issues raised
Action	Local branch managers	Practical things they need to do to prepare implementation timelines Where to go for support	Email	Change manager	Project sponsor, volunteer coordinator and project manager	One month before implementation	Branch managers to feedback how preparations are going

Audience: You need to be clear which stakeholder group each communication is aimed at. Some communications can go out to all stakeholders, but many will need to be tailored for different groups, depending on their roles and how the change will affect them. Tailoring may include changing the tone or terminology of the communications, the communications channel used, or focussing on different aspects of the change, for example different drivers and benefits, to appeal to particular stakeholder groups. Your stakeholder analysis (Chapter 4) can help to plan this.

Create and keep detailed lists of which stakeholders received which communication. This may seem very time consuming initially but will save confusion and mixed messaging, especially if plans are amended and you need to communicate out revisions and alterations. Creating mailing lists of stakeholder groups, such as change champions, middle managers, and project team members, can help save time and track who has received which communications.

Be mindful that not all members of the targeted stakeholder group may receive the communications as intended and plan additional communications activities as necessary. For example in the Workout! communications plan, the main communications activity for raising volunteers' interest in the change is the CEO's presentation at the annual conference. However, not all volunteers will attend the conference so some follow up communications activities will be needed. In this case, the business change manager emailed a summary of the CEO's presentation to all volunteers after the event and asked the branch managers to update any of their volunteers who did not attend.

Channel: The communications channel is how you choose to send your communication out, for example by email, presentation, intranet page, or face-to-face meeting. There are many channels to choose from, often categorised as one-way or two-way. You need to make sure you are using an appropriate channel for each of your communications.

One-way channels send communications out to recipients with no opportunity for them to respond, making them passive receivers of the information. One-way communications channels include intranet articles, information-only web pages, posters, all-staff emails, presentations, newsletters and newsletter articles, briefing notes for managers, Frequently Asked Questions (FAQs), and instruction manuals.

One-way channels enable information to be given out quickly to a wide audience whilst using minimal resources. They are best for disseminating simple information with very little complexity or room for misinterpretation. They are also good for high level messages about change initiatives, such as the drivers for the change and the expected benefits, to raise awareness and interest. If you are using one-way channels, always let people know where they can go to ask questions and obtain more information if they want to.

Two-way channels enable information to be given out to recipients and for them to respond, making them active participants in the communication. Two-way communications channels include face-to-face conversation, workshops, debates, telephone calls, email exchanges, social media, informal presentations, and lectures where there is the opportunity for open and honest discussion, team meetings, and classroom-based training sessions.

Two-way channels are best used when you need to give out complex or sensitive information and where there is lots of scope for misinterpretation and misunderstanding. As many two-way channels incorporate immediate feedback, they are good for communicating to challenging stakeholders, as reactions can be gauged and issues can be responded to instantly.

Two-way communications channels are far more resource intensive to use than one-way channels. Detailed preparation is needed to be able to tackle any immediate questions or issues, and further work will be required after the communication has been delivered to respond to feedback, research any issues which could not be resolved at the time, and keep recipients updated on the actions you have taken in light of their suggestions. Despite the extra effort needed, however, two-way channels are by far the best way to engage and increase the support of your users in any but the simplest and uncontentious of changes.

Three things to be aware of when choosing your communications channels

- A good approach to choosing your communications channels is to begin with one-way channels to raise awareness of the change and then use much richer, two-way channels as people move through interest into desire and action, where they will have much more involvement and engagement with the change on an individual level. The Workout! communication plan uses channels in this way.

  Be careful with this approach if your change is very sensitive, for example if it involves job losses or major changes to working conditions. In these cases, you can still announce the change through a one-way channel, but you will need to move quickly on to two-way channels, such as team meetings or one-to-one conversations, to give people the opportunity to ask questions and explore how the change will affect them before they have too much time to speculate and worry.

- If possible, use the communications channels that are already established in your organisation such as company intranets, regular newsletters, or staff forums. Most staff will be used to engaging with these channels and will see any information sent through them as legitimate. However, make sure you do not overestimate their reach. Just because an organisation posts information on an intranet site or sends an all-staff email doesn't mean that everyone reads it! (More information on corporate communications can be found later in the chapter.)

  You may need to complement established communications channels with more of your own, especially if the main channels used by the organisation are one-way. In some organisations, staff may not be used to two-way channels and suspicious of invitations to ask questions or give feedback. Clearly demonstrating how the information you gather from them is shaping your change, for example by amending the future product or processes on the basis of their feedback, will increase support for your change and give people confidence to engage with you further.

• If you are planning two-way communications activities, make sure the environment encourages genuine engagement. Very few people will feel comfortable asking difficult questions at the end of an all-staff CEO briefing or making controversial suggestions in front of their line manager or departmental head. In both cases, the risks of humiliation or being seen as a 'troublemaker' are too great. Line managers may also be constrained in front of their staff and not feel it is appropriate to be open and honest about the change with their team within earshot. Be very sensitive to hierarchical and societal norms and constraints within the organisation and make sure people are given the chance to interact freely without the fear of repercussions or negative consequences.

Box 8.1   Dealing with sensitive communications for Burntwood's EDRMS

The changes brought about by the Burntwood EDRMS programme would significantly affect both the technology and information management teams. There was a great deal of uncertainty and anxiety within the teams about how responsibilities, roles, and resources would be divided between them after implementation.

The business change manager was running a stakeholder mapping workshop and wanted to invite representatives from both the technology and information management teams. Neither of the representatives felt they could fully participate in the workshop in case they gave away any sensitive information or showed any weakness which could be used by the other to influence the future of their teams.

Therefore, the business change manager decided to run two workshops and invite one representative to each. In this way, each representative was willing to share vital information about stakeholders for the programme (on the understanding that nothing sensitive would be shared with the representative of the other team) and an uncomfortable and potentially damaging situation was avoided.

Sender: You need to decide who is the best person to deliver each of your communications. As a general rule, use your change sponsor for sending out important messages which need the attention of a wide range of stakeholders and local leaders and managers for more tailored team or department messages. Two-way communications are best delivered by yourself or close colleagues such as change champions, subject matter experts, or project team members, who know enough about the change to lead in-depth discussions and answer detailed questions, and whom you are confident will not give out erroneous information or promise things which cannot be delivered.

Be wary of any helpful sender who says that they can prepare and deliver their own communications about your change. Make sure you check everything for accuracy and consistency before it is delivered to minimise errors such as an over-enthusiastic change sponsor promising too much from the change or a project manager misunderstanding how an issue with implementation is being dealt with. Miscommunications are common when multiple people are sending messages and must be minimised to prevent confusion, unrealistic expectations, and subsequent disappointment for users.

Sign-off: Communicating accurate messages is extremely challenging in the complex and uncertain world of organisational change, so it is important that communications are agreed and signed off by all relevant people before being released into the organisation. As a minimum, you need sign-off from your change sponsor for any official or sensitive communications, but you will often need to get agreement from a wider range of key stakeholders including any senior leaders, managers, and project team members whose activities or roles relate to the messages. It is far better to spend more time getting agreement on your messages before sending out communications than dealing with the misunderstandings, negative reactions, and loss of trust which can be the result of sending out communications which key stakeholders do not know about or do not agree with.

You also need to think about anyone else who may need to be warned and briefed before the communication is sent. For example if your organisation is unionised, unions will need to be informed before communications about significant changes are sent to union members, and line managers will need to be briefed in order to answer any questions from their staff. In the Workout! communications plan, the volunteer coordinator is listed as someone who needs to agree and sign off all communications delivered to volunteers, as she will need to be able to answer questions and support volunteers who are affected by the change, even though she is not directly involved in planning or implementing the restructure herself.

Timing: When creating your communications plan, you should have an idea of when each of the communications will go out. However, you probably won't be able to finalise exact dates too far in advance, and even if you can, timelines for change initiatives alter frequently and rapidly. Be prepared to be flexible – put down expected dates to give you an idea of the flow of your communications plan and finalise them as your change progresses. Alternatively, you can create timings in relation to key milestones, for example 'two weeks before staff conference' or 'the day before implementation' and finalise dates as the milestones become clearer.

Make sure you differentiate between communication timings you can control and those which are fixed and immovable such as staff conferences, CEO presentations, or organisational newsletter publication dates. For these communication activities, the content of your message will have to reflect where you are in your change initiative at the time of the delivery, rather than timing the delivery to suit the messages you wish to give out.

Use the timings in your communications plan to check you are not going to clash with any other organisational communications, either for other change initiatives or for business as usual activities. This will help to avoid confusion and information overload for your users. For example no-one will take notice of a message about your computer upgrade change if it is sent out on the same day as a corporate message from the CEO about reductions to the annual leave allowance.

It can be tricky to decide when to communicate implementation dates for change initiatives. You need to give people enough notice to block out time in their diaries for training and other preparation and implementation activities, but many implementation schedules are finalised only very shortly before they commence. The more notice you can give users about implementation dates the better, but minimise potential irritation about delays by being clear that all implementation dates are subject to last minute changes. Let people know when dates will be finalised and send regular updates on progress in the meantime to keep interest levels high.

Measurement: Once you have delivered your communication to your stakeholders, you need to check that it has been received, read, and interpreted correctly, and any requested actions have been carried out.

There are a range of measurement methods to help you do this, including:

- Asking your local change champions to find out if their colleagues received the communication and check understanding of, and reaction to, the messages;
- Sending out short surveys to stakeholders to get feedback on various aspects of the communications such as clarity, ease of understanding, and effectiveness of channel;
- Asking champions or line managers to follow up on any requests for action to ensure they are completed;
- Giving a dedicated email address for people to feedback any thoughts or ideas following the communication. However, the feedback may be too sensitive to be written down, or people may mean to feedback but don't find the time to email, so couple this with more proactive feedback methods such as asking champions to gather feedback, to obtain a more accurate view.
- Employing software for sending out electronic newsletters that can report on how many recipients have accessed the information. This will give you an idea of the percentage of people who have seen your communication but not if they have read or understood it, so other methods will be needed to measure these.

Just as when measuring your change activities (discussed in Chapter 6), you will need to use a range of methods to understand how successful your communications are. The Workout! communications plan gives some ideas of how to use a range of methods depending on the type of communication delivered.

Making the most of corporate communications

Organisations communicate with their staff on a regular basis. Corporate information about regular performance results, important messages about strategy, staff changes and organisational policies, and organisation-wide learning and development interventions such as health and safety training need to reach all staff. Every organisation has a preferred way of communicating to their staff, and harnessing these corporate communications to send out messages about your change can be extremely helpful.

Whether your organisation uses an intranet, all-staff emails, staff newsletters, management cascade structures, all-staff briefings, or even just posters or notices on notice boards, communicating through these established mechanisms legitimises your change, giving out a clear signal that the change is official and endorsed by the leaders of the organisation. This will give staff confidence that the change is part of the organisation's strategy and the drivers for the change are genuine and significant. Conversely, an absence of information about your change in regular corporate communications may lead people to question how much of a priority the organisational leaders are placing on the change. Seeing information about the change in official corporate communications will also help to convince those in denial or disengaged that the change is actually going to happen and therefore they need to engage or be left behind.

Many larger organisations have corporate communications teams who are responsible for shaping and coordinating communications within and external to the organisation. If you have such a team in your organisation, they should be able to support your communication initiatives in a number of ways, including:

- Offering communications professionals to help develop your communications plan;
- Commenting on drafts of your communications;
- Offering advice on branding guidelines and communications channels;
- Owning and updating distribution lists;
- Letting you know when other communications are being sent out, so you can coordinate with other organisational messages;
- Owning specialist forums, for example manager forums and regular leadership meetings, where you may want to present information;
- Publishing information about your change through established channels, for example intranet sites and organisational newsletters;
- Leading on, or assisting with, any communications needed for stakeholders who are external to the organisation.

It is important to establish good relationships with any corporate communications teams. Meet with them regularly to update them on what you are doing and exchange information about what other communications are going out and harness any support or expertise they can offer you. This should really help you deliver effective communications which engage your users without overloading them with information and might significantly increase user attention and support towards your change.

Be careful, however, of assuming all staff engage with corporate communications channels. There will always be a proportion of staff who don't take any notice of corporate communications, however embedded the channels are. Make sure that you follow up on any corporate messages with other communications methods, for example asking your change champions to give out more information at regular team meetings following an announcement on the organisation's intranet. Also, bear in mind that many corporate communications channels are good for giving information out but not so good at encouraging questions or feedback. If this is the case in your organisation, make sure you couple the corporate messages with richer and more personal engagement activities to ensure your stakeholders are fully supported and engaged throughout the change journey.

Box 8.2   Using corporate communications during Spark Clearholme's office move

Spark Clearholme had a well-established intranet that was used for all corporate communications. The intranet was managed and run by a competent and efficient corporate communications team and accessed regularly by most staff. Therefore, the intranet was used as the main tool in building support for the office move through a series of corporate communications.

Attention was first drawn to the office move by a headline article on the intranet by the project sponsor, the Head of Facilities. Headline articles were an established way of getting key messages out the organisation and had a high readership rate.

Following this, a series of intranet pages was set up with more information about the move including the move schedule, photos of the new office space, answers to questions that had been asked during other engagement activities, and some of the key benefits of the move. Any other engagement activities about the move involved signposting users to these pages as a source of more information.

In the weeks running up to the move, instructions about how to prepare for the move, including checklists of how and what to pack and what to do with unwanted items, were developed and again put on the intranet. Once the move had taken place, welcome packs with instructions about where to find things such as stationery and how to carry out basic tasks such as booking meeting rooms were also produced and put on the intranet.

References and further reading

Fiske, J. 1996. *Introduction to Communication Studies*. 2nd ed. London: Routledge

Kotter, John P. 1996. *Leading Change*. Boston: Harvard Business School Press

Lewis, L. 2011. Organizational Change: Creating Change Through Strategic Communications. Chichester: Wiley-Blackwell

Sidhu, R. 2014. Communication and Engagement. In Smith, R., King, D., Sidhu, R. and Skelsey, D., eds. *The Effective Change Manager's Handbook*. London: Kogan Page, pp. 210–257

9 Learning and training

Organisational change, by its very definition, is about changing the way things are done. Therefore, learning to do things differently is a core requirement for most stakeholders, and organising learning and training interventions is commonly within the scope of the business change manager's role.

Providing learning and training interventions for your stakeholders, however, will not guarantee sustainable change. Learning is a personal process which occurs over time and with experience and will vary for every individual stakeholder depending on their personalities and circumstances, their motivations to engage in the learning process, and their levels of experience and confidence in both learning itself and the subject of each particular learning situation.

Your job as a change manager is to encourage your stakeholders to engage in the learning process and offer relevant and useful interventions to help them. You cannot force them to learn, only encourage and support them in their learning process and make it as easy as possible for them to become skilful and confident in the new ways of doing things.

There are many types of learning interventions, including classroom-based training sessions, e-learning modules, written instructions, and one-to-one support. You need to choose the best interventions for each situation, depending on the types and levels of learning required and the needs of your stakeholders.

Business change managers are not necessarily expected to be learning and development experts. Designing, delivering, and evaluating workplace training and learning is a professional discipline, normally found within Learning and Development or HR departments. However, you do need to know enough to ensure that your learning interventions are suitable and as effective as possible. In order to do this, there are three elements you need to consider:

1   Who needs to learn something new, and what do they need to learn?
2   What type of learning interventions are needed?
3   How are you going to know if the learning intervention was successful?

Let's explore each of these elements in more detail.

Who needs to learn something new, and what do they need to learn?

Anyone who needs to do anything differently as a direct or indirect consequence of your change needs to learn what they need to do after the change has been implemented.

As well as your end users, don't forget any support functions who may also need to learn how to do new things. For example if you are putting in a new piece of software, the technology teams who are installing and looking after the software will need to be trained in how to do this. If you have a technology support desk that will be the first point of call for users, they will also need to be trained in what the software does and the common things that might go wrong.

Your stakeholder analysis (Chapter 4) and impact assessment (Chapter 6) will help you to identify the people who will need to do something different as part of your change and who will therefore need learning interventions to support them.

Box 9.1   Using the 7S model to identify learning needs for Burntwood's EDRMS

The 7S impact assessment for Burntwood is illustrated in Chapter 3. Impacts in six out of the seven organisational aspects identified changes which necessitated at least one stakeholder group having to learn to do things differently. These learning needs are summarised in Table 9.1. Each separate learning need will require an appropriate learning intervention.

Table 9.1 Learning needs for Burntwood's EDRMS

7S Area	Stakeholder Group	Learning Need
Structure	Local information champions	Undertaking new role of supporting teams to manage information
	Centralised information management team	Supporting local information champions and team leaders to manage their information
Systems	Technology staff	Installing, maintaining, and supporting the EDRMS within Burntwood's existing technology structures
Style	Team leaders	Responsibility and accountability for team's information management
Staff	All staff	Managing information as a core competence
Skills	All staff	Using the EDRMS, managing information well, and understanding and adhering to information management policies
Shared Values	All staff	A move to understanding, believing, and acting upon the following values: • Individuals and teams respect and comply with centrally created policies for collective good, • Individual achievement comes from working with others for increased success of organisation, • Administrative tasks are everyone's responsibility.

What type of learning interventions are needed?

Choosing which learning interventions to use depends on a number of factors, including:

- How great a change the new ways of working will be;
- Whether the change affects behaviours and cultures;
- How much support or resistance there is towards the change;
- How much resource you have to develop and deliver learning interventions;
- Whether there are any learning, training, or support materials already available;
- What training methods are common within the organisation;
- What the organisation will tolerate in terms of disruption to business as usual.

There are a number of established learning interventions that can be used. The following are five of the most popular.

Classroom-based training

This is the classic learning intervention where users gather in a room and receive training from an expert trainer. Training can also take place virtually, using remote conferencing technology such as Skype or WebEx.

Classroom-based training is good for explaining how to use complex new products and processes as learners can try things out in a safe environment and ask as many questions as necessary. The intervention can also be used to introduce new cultures and behaviours, but additional learning interventions such as longer term one-to-one support will also be needed to ensure that these deep and fundamental changes are successfully embedded.

Classroom-based training is a rich communications channel (see Chapter 8 for more information on communications channels), so can be used to increase support and buy-in for your change, explore potential benefits, and answer queries and concerns. Therefore, it can be a good intervention when resistance is high or users are not particularly engaged.

Classroom-based training is time consuming and resource intensive to arrange and run. Training rooms, materials, equipment, and trainers need to be organised and users have to be booked onto sessions. Every user has to take time out of their business as usual work to attend. To get an idea of how disruptive this can be, when 1,500 users attended a half day training course for Burntwood's EDRMS it was the equivalent of losing 750 days, or over 2 years, of a full-time business as usual role. Users have to attend training sessions at a particular time and place, which may mean colleagues have to cover their business as usual activities, and additional sessions usually need to be arranged to cover absence through illness, annual leave, and last minute emergencies. Training sessions are usually one-off events, so it is difficult for users to revisit if questions arise after the training has finished. This can be overcome by accompanying the sessions with written materials, e-learning, or floorwalking to ensure users continue to be supported after the training sessions have finished.

Box 9.2   Classroom-based training for Burntwood's EDRMS

Every staff member in Burntwood County Council would have to use the EDRMS to manage their electronic information. They also needed to learn the new information management policies and unfamiliar behaviours such as taking responsibility for their own information and seeing information management as part of their core role.

The EDRMS was quite complex to use properly, the expected behaviours were not universally popular, and limited enthusiasm had been shown for the change amongst the majority of users. Burntwood had a well-established culture of classroom-based training and the third-party EDRMS supplier could provide the necessary training materials. Therefore, the business change manager decided that classroom-based training, accompanied by written instructions and floorwalking, would be the most appropriate learning intervention.

The training material from the third-party supplier was amended to contain Burntwood terminology and use familiar scenarios that users would trust and understand. Alongside this, the new policies were introduced and necessary changes to behaviours and culture discussed within the session. A selection of champions signed off the training session before it was rolled out during implementation.

After the training, each user was supported by their user support officer and local champion through implementation and the early days of the change. There were also printed instruction manuals and quick crib sheets for the most commonly occurring tasks, which were available in hard copy and on the intranet. The monthly internal newsletter also published 'EDRMS Tip of the Month', covering best practice suggestions developed by champions and user support officers.

E-learning

E-learning encompasses any pre-prepared and recorded training carried out via electronic media, including interactive training modules and instructional videos.

E-learning is very good for learning how to use less complex products and follow simpler processes. It can be accessed by large amounts of users at the same time and is very flexible in that users can undertake the e-learning at their own pace and at a time and location of their choice. Users can also revisit any part of the training at future points, for example as a refresher during the first few weeks of implementation. It is less resource intensive to deliver than classroom-based training, and it is very easy to keep a record of who has accessed and completed the training.

Given the leaner communications channel, e-learning is not so effective for explaining complicated instructions or training in processes where ambiguity is present or complex decision making is needed. It is also very limited in its ability to help in instances of behavioural or cultural change. As there is no immediate feedback or discussion possible during the intervention, it is also of minimal use for increasing buy-in by discussing drivers and benefits or enabling recipients to ask questions and raise issues. It can be resource intensive to develop, especially if your organisation does not have any e-learning provision already set up. All e-learners will need easy access to an electronic device, and always provide headphones to computer-based workers who need to undertake e-learning.

E-learning technology is in constant development, and it is continually becoming a richer, more interactive learning intervention. If you work in an organisation which embraces and invests in e-learning – both the technology and the expertise to develop effective materials – you may find that the scope for using e-learning for complex changes and challenging stakeholders is far greater than for organisations which only have a basic provision.

Box 9.3   E-learning for Spark and Clearholme's marketing campaign planner

The introduction of the marketing campaign planner was a modest change for Spark and Clearholme. All marketing officers would be required to enter their marketing data into one central system, whereas currently there were lots of systems in use, from spreadsheets to scraps of paper. However, the new system was quite straightforward and the change offered enough benefits for the marketing officers to be enthusiastic and supportive. After implementation, management reports would be created weekly from the data entered into the software, so any errors or omissions would easily be identified and additional targeted support could be given.

Marketing officers worked flexible hours and travelled away from the office regularly, so attending classroom-based training would be difficult. Spark and Clearholme's Learning and Development department had recently begun providing e-learning for corporate training which had been very popular with staff. They had the technology and the expertise to produce and run more e-learning and were very keen to embed the learning intervention within the organisation.

The business change manager decided to offer short e-learning videos as the main learning intervention for the marketing campaign planner, with additional support from a network of super users. He worked closely with the e-learning expert in Learning and Development to produce a short series of videos, each explaining one feature of the planner. The information for these was adapted from the training manual provided by the third-party software provider and tips on best practice from the super users who had tested the software and knew its capabilities. The super users signed off the videos before they were launched.

No video was more than two minutes long, and videos were accessed through Spark and Clearholme's intranet. The videos could be accessed on computers, laptops, tablets, and smartphones at any time. Therefore, users could access exactly the information they needed at the time they needed it, in a variety of locations. After implementation, super users were available to provide extra support for individuals either face to face or through email or telephone if the user was away from the office. The marketing manager took responsibility for examining the management reports every week to check for errors or omissions and informed the relevant super user if anyone needed extra support.

Written instructions

Written instructions include training manuals, instruction emails, crib sheets (concise sets of notes used for quick reference), and any other written materials explaining how to do things. These can be printed in hard copy or made available online.

Written instructions are very useful for explaining specific steps needed to use a product or carry out a process. Visuals such as diagrams and screenshots can be used to illustrate the written information, making it even easier for people to follow. They can be accessed by users at any time and worked through at an individual pace. They can be revisited as often as necessary so are good for backing up other interventions such as classroom-based training sessions. Written instructions are not too resource intensive to produce or disseminate and can be used by a wide range of people simultaneously. They can also be easily tailored for different groups of users.

Written instructions can only contain limited information before they become very complicated, so are not very effective where there is ambiguity or a need for complex decision making or for cultural and behavioural changes. They are not interactive so users will not be able to ask questions, explore issues, or discuss the reasons for the change whilst using them. Therefore, make sure the materials contain information about where to get further support if needed. Once written instructions are printed they are difficult to update, and it is challenging to control the versions that people have access to. This can be made easier if the date and version is displayed clearly on all printed materials, so users can see if the instructions they are using are the most recent.

Box 9.4   Written materials for the Spark Clearholme office move

There were very few cultural and behaviour changes needed for Spark Clearholme's office move. Most of the changes concerned simple and practical information such as where to find new meeting rooms, where the teams were located, and how to use the new photocopiers and printers. None of these were huge differences to current ways of working. There were very little resources available for developing learning interventions, and written materials such as floor maps showing meeting rooms, team seating plans, and instructions for photocopiers and printers were already available.

Therefore, the main learning intervention consisted of producing clear written instructions and maps and posting them on Spark Clearholme's intranet, which was very well used by staff. All instructions were read and agreed by the relocation group (the network of change champions) before being published. The instructions were also printed out and placed on each new desk as part of a welcome pack, along with discount vouchers for the new café, instructions on how to register to join the new gym, and a list of Frequently Asked Questions which had been gathered by the relocation group over the previous few weeks.

Floorwalkers from the technology department visited each desk on the first morning of the move to check that everyone's computers were working properly. The relocation group members from each department supported their colleagues for the first few days and directed them to the intranet for further information when necessary. They also gathered any new questions and issues raised by their colleagues and fed them back to the business change manager. Users reported that the move went smoothly and they felt well supported by the floorwalkers and relocation group and had enough written information to make all the changes that they needed to in order to settle down in the new building.

Super users and floorwalking

As discussed in Chapter 7, change champions are nominated users who work with the business change manager to support their colleagues to accept and adopt the change. Super users play a slightly different but complementary role, becoming an expert in any new products and processes needed for your change and specifically supporting users to learn to operate them. Champions or other nominated users can play this role, as can subject matter experts, technology support staff, or third-party suppliers. Super users can help with testing new products and processes and supporting users during implementation as they learn to work in new ways.

Floorwalking is when champions or super users visit users during and after implementation to check that they are confident in the new ways of working, answer any questions or queries, deal with any issues, and provide additional learning support if necessary. The visits can be arranged to be suitable for both users and floorwalkers. For example the IT specialist floorwalkers for Spark Clearholme's office move visited each desk on the first day after the move to check that all the technology was working, whereas the relocation group, whose members were all part of teams which had moved, offered longer term support in a more informal manner. They had casual conversations with colleagues in coffee breaks and over lunch to check everything was working well and had a brief slot at weekly team meetings to pick up any issues from their teams and feedback any new information from the office move project team. They continued with the role until they felt that their teams had settled in sufficiently to no longer need their support.

Floorwalking is a good learning intervention for users who want to ask specific questions and try things out in real life but with the safety of an expert on hand. It enables learners to learn at their own pace and focus on specific areas of the change that they may be struggling with. Floorwalking can be continued for as long as necessary (providing the resource is available), so can really help with consolidating learning and embedding the change. More information about floorwalking is given in Chapter 10.

Due to the personal nature of the intervention, and the fact that the floorwalker visits the user in their normal place of work, floorwalking is very good for making users feel supported and safe. Individual issues can be dealt with very quickly, and best practice ideas can be picked up from individuals and shared with other users. Therefore, floorwalking can work well for changes where there is ambiguity or complex decision making, where processes could not be completely defined before implementation, or where behavioural change is required.

Floorwalking can be very resource intensive, either by procuring subject matter experts or taking super users and champions away from their business as usual demands. Therefore, the intervention is often used to support other learning activities such as classroom-based training or e-learning, rather than as a stand-alone intervention, enabling the floorwalkers to focus on any users needing extra support to make the change.

One-to-one support

This intervention includes coaching, mentoring, personal training, and on the job learning supported by the line manager.

One-to-one support is very effective for encouraging behavioural change and focussing on wider cultural issues. It tends to be a longer-term intervention over a number of weeks or months and can tackle very sensitive and challenging issues around change. The personal nature of the intervention encourages users to ask questions, explore complexities and ambiguities, experiment with new behaviours in a safe environment, and take responsibility for their personal development.

Given the intensive nature of the intervention, both in resources and approach, one-to-one support is generally used sparingly and targeted for individuals who will make the biggest impact through working in the new ways. To be an effective coach or mentor requires training in itself so you need to have access to professionals in the field or ensure that the line managers are comfortable in undertaking the role.

Box 9.5   One-to-one support for leaders during the Spark Clearholme finance department restructure

After the leadership team had agreed the necessary culture changes needed in Spark Clearholme's finance department (see Chapter 2 for more information), they decided to lead the change from the top by ensuring all their actions and decisions reflected the new culture they desired for the department.

To help with this, the department director and his three direct reports undertook individual coaching from a trusted coach who knew them and supported the culture they were trying to achieve. During the coaching, they each focussed on specific scenarios they were facing and explored how to approach and manage differently on the basis of the new cultures and behaviours.

Soon the new behaviours became noticeable to the rest of the leadership team, who began to follow their example, discussing and exploring their own scenarios and behaviours amongst themselves. The leadership team also pledged to support one other by flagging up signs of old behaviours and working together to rectify them. After a few months, all the leadership team were beginning to think in line with the desired cultures and much less in the old ways. By becoming comfortable and confident in the new behaviours and cultures themselves first, the leadership team were then able to cascade the changes throughout the rest of the department, supporting their staff to make the changes whilst continuing to lead by example.

How are you going to know if the learning intervention was successful?

Successful completion of a one-off learning intervention does not necessarily mean that meaningful and sustainable learning has taken place. To illustrate this, take a look at Figure 9.1, the evaluation results for the classroom-based training sessions for Mayer & Co's e-file implementation.

As you can see from the answers, the training itself was very well received, with the vast majority of users reporting that they understood and found it useful. However, only 30% of users were confident that they could use the new system following the training. The learning intervention itself could be said to be successful but did not in itself complete the individual learning process for the users. Further learning interventions were required before users were confident to make the change and embedded the new ways of working successfully.

To be confident that your users are really learning successfully, you need to measure each individual user's progress over time rather than focussing on

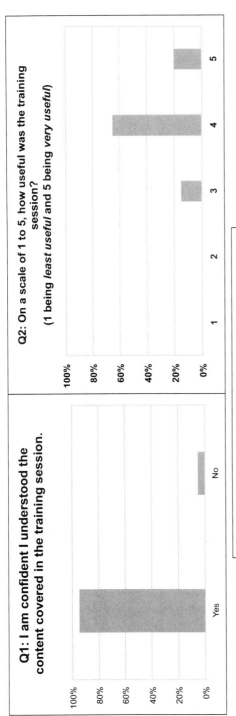
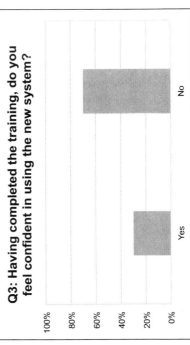

Figure 9.1 Evaluation results for Mayer & Co e-file classroom–based training

measuring the impact of each separate learning intervention. Only when each individual user is confidently and consistently working in the new ways can you be sure that their learning process has been completed.

Box 9.6   Measuring successful learning for Mayer & Co's e-file

To monitor each user's progress through the learning process, and therefore measure the overall success of the learning interventions for Mayer & Co's e-file, the business change manager developed individual progress sheets for each user. Success was mainly demonstrated through informal observation and discussion with the user by the relevant assessor, and the progress sheets were used to decide when to move each team from project support into business as usual (see Chapter 11 for more details on this).

Table 9.2 is an example of one user's progress sheet showing a successfully completed learning process.

Table 9.2 Learning progress sheet for Mayer & Co e-file

Learning Intervention	Assessor	Completed	Success Demonstrated	Details of Further Support Accessed
Attend classroom-based training session	Trainer	Y	Y	
Receive training manual and link to online support materials	Champion	Y	Y	
Floorwalker visit week 1	Champion	Y	N	Champion talked through the training manual and supported user to undertake basic e-file review
Floorwalker visit week 2	Champion	Y	Y	User comfortable in undertaking basic e-file review
Floorwalker visit week 4	Champion	Y	N	Champion talked through more advanced functions of e-file with reference to training manual and online material. Agreed repeat visit next week to check progress.
Line manager review at three months	Line manager	Y	N	User undertaking file reviews well but lacks confidence in more advanced tasks not repeated regularly. Contacted super user to arrange a support session.
Line manager review at six months	Line manager	Y	Y	Regular support from super user has resulted in confident and successful use of e-file for all necessary tasks.

References and further reading

Canadian Literacy and Learning Network. 2016. [online] Available at: <www.literacy.ca/professionals/professional-development-2/principles-of-adult-learning/> [Accessed 24 March 2016]

Knowles, M., Holton, E. and Swanson, R. 2005. *The Adult Learner: The Definitive Classic in Adult Education and Human Resource Development*. 6th ed. Burlington: Elsevier

Senge, P., Roberts, C., Ross, R., Smith, B., Roth, G. and Kleiner, A. 1999. *The Dance of Change*. London: Nicholas Brealey Publishing

Smith, R. 2014. Education and Learning Support. In Smith, R., King, D., Sidhu, R. and Skelsey, D., eds. *The Effective Change Manager's Handbook*. London: Kogan Page, pp. 367–414

Part three

Implementing and sustaining change

10 Supporting your users through implementation

There are three common ways of introducing, or implementing, change into organisations:

1   'Big bang' implementation
2   Phased implementation
3   Parallel running.

Each has different advantages and disadvantages for users, as explored in the following sections.

'Big bang' implementation

This is where all change happens at once. One day things are done in the old way, and the next day things are done in the new way. For example moving everyone from one office building to another over a weekend, so everyone packs up and leaves their old office on a Friday and starts work in their new office on a Monday.

Advantages

- It gives a very clear ending to old ways of working so all users can focus completely on getting used to the new.
- All the changes are made at the same time, minimising confusion for users about what has changed at any one point and what has yet to change.
- The implementation period is short so everyone involved, including leaders, managers, and users, should be able to maintain focus and keep it as a top priority.

Disadvantages

- It can be resource intensive to provide adequate support for users if all implementation activities take place at the same time.
- If there are issues in the early days of implementation, all users will be affected. This may cause a significant impact on the organisation and result in many dissatisfied users.

- There is no opportunity to try out any implementation activities with smaller groups of users in advance so there is only one chance to get it right.

Box 10.1 'Big bang' restructure for Spark Clearholme's finance department

During the merger of Spark Clearholme, the finance teams from both pre-merger businesses were restructured to form one finance department. After months of preparation, interviews, internal recruitment, training, and job shadowing, all staff moved into their new roles on the same day.

The 'big bang' approach to the restructure gave a clear cutover point for the department, minimising confusion about whether people were in old or new roles. Everyone could settle into their new roles quickly and concentrate on building new working relationships and refining new ways of working with the minimum of interim arrangements. Information about the new structure and key contacts within the department could be disseminated to the rest of the organisation in one go, minimising confusion and misunderstanding for anyone who needed to contact the department.

Despite the months of preparation, some external recruitment had not been completed by the implementation date. This meant some people had to undertake interim line management and additional tasks after implementation until all roles had been filled. The first few weeks after implementation were hard work for the department as people learned their new jobs and built new relationships. There was a tendency for some staff to rely quite heavily on colleagues who had previously filled their role, but this reduced as confidence grew. Three months after implementation, the department completed its first set of organisational accounts, and the leadership team provided cakes for everyone to celebrate the success.

Phased implementation

Change is introduced in smaller chunks, and the change takes a while to be fully introduced. For example moving one team over to a new computer system every fortnight until all teams have made the change.

Advantages

- Enthusiastic users can go first. They are more likely to be tolerant of early issues and good experiences can be used to increase the interest and confidence of their more sceptical colleagues.
- Lessons can be learned about both the change itself and the way the change is being implemented from early phases, resulting in a better experience for later recipients.
- More focused support can be given to smaller numbers of users for each phase of the change.

Disadvantages

- As users move from old ways of working to new at different times, it can be confusing for users and may create the need for extra activities until implementation is complete.
- Any unhappiness during early implementation can spread to later recipients, reducing support and, if many issues arise, potentially delaying or stopping the change completely.
- Disruption and uncertainty lasts for longer and benefits may not be realised until implementation is complete.

Box 10.2   Phased implementation at Workout!

The Workout! restructure involved amalgamating 150 local branches into 60 employment service areas (ESAs). A new role of ESA assistant was created for each ESA to arrange and book training sessions for employment seekers, and a new course booking and finance system was introduced.

Initially, a pilot was run by amalgamating four enthusiastic branches into one ESA. During the pilot, more details were learned about the skills and knowledge needed by the ESA assistant, and some small amendments were made to the booking and finance system. Customers from the pilot area were soon reporting increased satisfaction with the service they were receiving.

The main implementation was carried out in six phases, creating ten ESAs per phase. The phases each took four months, giving one month for recruitment and preparation and then three months for implementation and initial embedding. After this, providing there were no outstanding issues, management of the ESAs was passed to a business as usual operations manager. Users in the first phase contacted the pilot ESA to learn about their experiences and were pleased to hear about the improved customer services. The pilot ESA assistant supported her newly recruited colleagues during phase one and good news stories from both the pilot and the first phase were captured and disseminated to the other branches to help raise their enthusiasm for the change. Two years later, all sixty ESAs had been created and were running successfully.

Parallel running

Users work in both the new ways and the old ways for a period of time. For example financial information would be entered into both an old and new accounting system for a number of weeks until the old system is switched off. Parallel running can be used with both 'big bang' and phased approaches.

Advantages

- It can give stakeholders more confidence in making the change because the old ways of working are still in operation.
- It gives users the chance to try out the new ways of working with significantly reduced risk that errors will disrupt key activities.
- Old ways of working are stopped only when everyone is happy that the new ways are working, giving users as much time as they need to make the transition.

Disadvantages

- Tasks need to be done twice, in both the old and the new ways. This is inefficient and may confuse and irritate users.
- Most change is very messy and uncomfortable for a while. Keeping old ways of working available may increase the desire to give up the change before it has a chance to succeed.
- Minor issues could delay the decision to stop parallel running, leaving users to work in both old and new ways unnecessarily.

Box 10.3   Parallel running for Spark Clearholme's marketing campaign planner

The marketing campaign planner had a phased implementation, with each of Spark Clearholme's ten marketing teams receiving the new software at fortnightly intervals. The biggest risk with the implementation was the switch from recording campaign finances in the corporate finance system to entering and managing it in the new planner. If any errors occurred whilst moving the data, or problems arose with the planner, all of Spark Clearholme's financial planning and reporting may be affected.

Therefore, users continued to enter financial data in the corporate system as well as the new planner for one month after implementation. This gave them time to get used to the new ways of working whilst minimising the risk to the wider organisation. If, after the first month, all the finances in the planner were correct and the users were confident with the new ways of working, they moved solely to working in the planner. If there were any issues during the first month, users continued with the parallel running whilst receiving more support and training. Parallel running meant that users had to enter the same information into two systems, so their managers made sure they were given extra time to complete this. The business change manager arranged a thank you party for all affected users at the end of the implementation to recognise the extra effort they made during the implementation.

Preparing for implementation

Making the decision to go ahead with implementation is a very big milestone in the change journey. Suddenly, everything becomes real – the impacts of the change are about to be felt, the risks of failure move closer, and your change sponsor and other senior leaders are about to find out if months, if not years, of preparation will result in a change which works well enough to realise its expected benefits. It is the moment when concept becomes reality, and the pressures felt on those responsible for the change can be enormous.

Given the immensity of the decision, you need to provide your decision makers with evidence that the organisation is fully prepared and ready for the change. This is normally done through a business readiness assessment.

Completing a business readiness assessment

The business readiness assessment is a checklist of all the preparation needed by stakeholders in order for the organisation to be ready to commence implementation of the change. It is evidence for your key decision makers that the organisation is ready for the change and will help them to make the decision to start the implementation.

Before they agree to start implementing, your decision makers will need to be confident that their operational leaders and managers are happy to instigate and support the change. In their turn, the operational leaders and managers will need to be confident that their staff are happy to make the effort to change their ways of working. You can help to show this by asking each stakeholder group to endorse their section of the business readiness assessment as an indication that they are ready to change.

Table 10.1 shows the business readiness assessment for Mayer & Co's E-file implementation. It consists of a series of statements for each stakeholder group

Table 10.1 Business readiness assessment for Mayer & Co e-file

Stakeholder Group	Readiness Statement	Sign-Off
Leaders	Leaders are able to articulate the benefits of e-file to their colleagues and staff	All department heads
	Leaders have attended a demonstration and facilitated discussion about e-file	
	Leaders understand and agree to the changes e-file will bring to the organisation and their particular areas of responsibility	
	Leaders understand the implementation approach and the role they, their managers, and change champions will play	
	The impacts of releasing staff from business as usual for training is understood	
	Leaders are aware of how they and their staff will be supported throughout implementation, including how to give feedback	

(Continued)

Table 10.1 (Continued)

Stakeholder Group	Readiness Statement	Sign-Off
	Leaders are aware of how success of the implementation will be measured	
	Leaders are aware of the roll back approach (if problems occur during implementation) and what will trigger it	
	The potential impacts of the implementation on short-term productivity is understood and adjustments in place as needed	
	Leaders have no outstanding concerns which they believe should delay the implementation of e-file	
Team Managers	Team managers are able to articulate the benefits of e-file to their teams	Nominated team managers (two per department)
	Teams have attended a demonstration and facilitated discussion about e-file	
	Team managers understand and agree to the changes in e-file will bring to themselves and their teams	
	Team managers understand the implementation approach and the role they, their teams, and change champions will play	
	All team members are signed up to a scheduled training session	
	The impacts of releasing staff out of business as usual for training is understood and alternatives put in place if needed	
	Team managers are aware of how they and their teams will be supported throughout implementation, including how to give feedback	
	Team managers are aware of how success of the implementation will be measured	
	Team managers are aware of the roll back approach (if problems occur during implementation) and what will trigger it	
	The potential impacts of the implementation on short-term productivity is understood and adjustments in place as needed	
	Team managers have no outstanding concerns which they believe should delay the implementation of e-file	
Change Champions	All change champions understand their role in the implementation of e-file	Nominated change champions (two per department)
	All change champions are adequately trained and supported to carry out their role	
	Change champions understand how communications will work between them and the project team	
	Change champions have agreed how to communicate and gather feedback from their teams	
	Change champions understand the implementation approach and the roll back approach and their role in each	
	All trainers are trained and prepared and ready to commence	
	Change champions have no outstanding concerns which they believe should delay the implementation of e-file	

which were signed by representatives from these groups to signal that all users were ready to make the change from working with paper files to electronic files. A specific 'go/no go' meeting was arranged where the assessment was presented to the project sponsor and board by the departmental heads, who gave their verbal support for the commencement of the implementation. At this meeting, the heads were also able to answer any additional queries the decision makers had about how they would manage implementation in their local areas.

Managing the first few weeks of implementation

The period of implementation and the weeks following can often feel chaotic and out of control. Despite how much planning and preparation you have done, you may still feel like you have unleashed a wild beast into the organisation and it is running amok causing untold harm and refusing to be tamed. Issues you may find yourself facing include:

- Limitless queries from increasingly irritable users, all of which need answering;
- Impacted activities which were not picked up before implementation, which need investigation and action;
- Unforeseen consequences and problems with the change, needing investigation, fixes, and temporary workarounds;
- Rumours, speculation, and erroneous information flying about, which needs curbing and rectifying;
- Annoyed champions being blamed by unhappy colleagues, who need placating;
- Project teams juggling and prioritising endless issues, requests, and demands, who need information and decisions;
- Managers and staff pushing to halt the change, who need encouragement and hope;
- Leaders on the verge of panic, who need confidence and reassurance;
- Exhausted colleagues, leaders, and stakeholders, who have burnt themselves out preparing for the change without realising that this is where the hard work starts!

The most important thing to realise at this point is that the pain of implementation is normal. It is much, much worse if you are underprepared, but it is very rare for any significant implementation to be painless. Rosabeth Moss Kanter, a Harvard professor in organisational change, has even developed a law about this stage. Known as Kanter's Law, it states 'Everything looks like a failure in the middle' (Kanter, 2009).

It is vital not to be defeated by this stage. As Kanter goes on to say: 'But stop the effort too soon, and by definition it is a failure. Stay with it through its hurdles, make appropriate adjustments, and you could be on the way to success.'

So what can you do to manage the pain of implementation and move through as quickly as possible to a more settled and positive future? Following are some ideas on how to deal with issues and feedback from users, manage the performance dip, and support your leaders through this tricky period.

Dealing with user queries

There will be lots of queries from your users for at least a few weeks after implementation. You need a robust system in place to deal with these; otherwise, it can easily become overwhelming and unmanageable. Questions may go unanswered and feedback unacknowledged, or erroneous information may be given out by well-meaning but ill-informed supporters. This will all lead to frustration amongst your users and rapidly decreasing support for the new ways of working.

One way to avoid this is to collect and manage queries through one central point – usually yourself as the business change manager. This minimises the risk of losing anything and ensures that issues and queries can be forwarded onto the correct people and responses to the users can be managed and controlled. In addition, you will quickly gain an oversight of key themes and issues coming in from users, even if the feedback is coming from disparate parts of the organisation.

The example in Box 10.4 shows how the business change manager at Mayer & Co organised and managed user queries for the first few weeks of the e-file implementation.

Box 10.4   Managing user queries at Mayer & Co

The e-file champions were responsible for gathering all queries from their colleagues during the e-file implementation at Mayer & Co. They had all attended training sessions and practised using e-file in advance so they were confident in helping colleagues who were struggling to use the system. If users had queries that the champions could not answer immediately, they made a note of them and promised to find out more.

The business change manager held a debriefing session every afternoon with the champions to discuss the types of queries that had arisen that day. If lots of users had raised queries about similar activities that had been covered in training, the business change manager took away a task to create simple crib sheets (concise sets of quick reference notes) for these activities. The champions gave these out to all their users to pre-empt anyone else struggling with the same issues.

Users also asked the champions questions which had not been covered in training. These queries tended to fall into four main categories:

1   Previously unknown features of the system,
2   Suggested best practice discovered through experimentation,

3   Issues with local ways of working which had not been investigated before implementation,

4   Actual issues with the e-file system – bugs or errors.

The business change manager filtered these queries out to the appropriate people for investigation. Her technology colleagues dealt with the bugs and errors, subject matter experts investigated unknown features and suggested best practice to see whether it added value and should be adopted by other users, and team managers were informed of any local ways of working which needed amending to fit with e-file. Everyone fed progress back to the business change manager, who issued updates to the champions every day so they could keep users informed. The business change manager also issued weekly updates to the project sponsor and department heads so they were aware of what issues were being raised and how they were being dealt with.

Managing the performance dip

When change is implemented into an organisation, a short-term decline in performance often occurs as people get used to working in new ways. This is perfectly normal, but if people are not expecting it it's easy for them to panic, thinking that the change has failed as things are taking longer than they were before. More pressure can be put on staff to work harder at a time when they are physically and emotionally adjusting to the change, and confidence and morale can drop very quickly.

Therefore, you will need to prepare both your users and your senior leaders for the possibility of a short-term dip in performance during implementation. It is not usually possible to calculate exactly how big the dip will be and how long it will last, as there is no accurate way of measuring in advance how much time people will need to adjust to the change. However, a working assumption can be made that the bigger the change is from the current ways of working, the greater the performance drop will probably be.

Offering users lots of training and support and ensuring any issues and feedback is gathered and acted upon quickly will help to minimise the performance dip in the early days of implementation. If possible, agree in advance with your senior leaders to relax any performance-related targets during implementation. For example the department heads at Mayer & Co reduced caseworkers' targets by 20% for the first four weeks of the e-file implementation to give users a chance to get used to the new ways of working. Temporary staff were brought in to help review urgent cases during this time to ensure customers were not impacted by the change.

Supporting your leaders when everything is messy and uncomfortable

One of the biggest challenges in the first few weeks of go live can be ensuring that your leaders keep calm and continue to support the change without faltering, wavering, or losing confidence. If they are experienced in leading change, they will be calmer and more able to cope with this stage, but if not, this can be a very scary and uncertain time. They are responsible if the change fails, and it is easy for them to panic during the early days when lots of issues may be arising and performance deteriorating.

Following are a few suggestions for managing your leaders through the first few weeks of implementation when things can be really messy and uncomfortable.

- **Prepare them in advance:** Describe what the early days of implementation may feel like and reassure them of the processes you have put in place to manage user issues. Invite leaders from other organisations who have led similar changes to come and talk to your leaders about what happened during the implementation and how they handled it.
- **Keep focussed on the facts:** Leaders will hear far more negative feedback from unhappy people than neutral or positive feedback from those who are coping better with the change. Ensure you regularly update them with objective feedback, facts, and measurements to give them a true idea of the state of the change.
- **Be honest about what is happening:** If issues and problems are encountered in the early weeks of the implementation – and they often are – use your leaders to break down any barriers and release any resources necessary to investigate and overcome the issues. Book regular meetings into your leaders' diaries in advance so you don't have to try to schedule urgent meetings at the last minute – you can always cancel them nearer the time if they are not needed.
- **Keep them calm:** You need your leaders to be rational, objective, and impartial during this stage of the change. If they panic, they will begin to act emotionally which will not help if they are called on to make difficult decisions or take unpopular actions. Keep all language unemotive and objective in reports and emails and during meetings and discussions. Try to avoid situations where people begin to blame each other for problems – encourage everyone to work together to solve issues and get the change working. There will be plenty of time to hold reviews on what went wrong when things have settled down.
- **Remind your leaders how far they have come:** It is easy to achieve something and then just dismiss it and move onto the next problem. Take time to acknowledge milestones and achievements as you go through the implementation to boost morale and give a sense of perspective of the size of the current problems against the size of what is being achieved overall.
- **Focus on the vision:** Regularly remind your leaders of the compelling future that will be possible only if the change is made. This vision of a better future is what everyone signed up to and have been working so hard to achieve – getting there will be worth all the current pain and anguish.
- **Find and advertise early quick wins and good news stories:** Use champions to pick up where people are beginning to see immediate benefits

or the potential for benefits in the future. Look for pockets of positivity – they will be there somewhere! Use these examples to keep spirits high until things begin to embed and settle down.

Box 10.5   A quick win at Burntwood County Council

One of the first teams to go live with the EDRMS at Burntwood County Council was the organisation-wide procurement team. Traditionally, as there had been no secure way of sharing electronic documents across the organisation, all documents for every procurement activity – hundreds each year – had to be printed out and delivered by hand to the relevant departments. Not only did this mean that the small, overstretched procurement team had to spend a lot of time printing out documents, but they then had to deliver them by hand to the teams, regardless of where they were located.

After the EDRMS implementation, the procurement team was able to share the documents with the relevant departments electronically. Not only did this save them many hours a day, it dramatically reduced printing costs and environmental savings due to the reduced paper usage. The business change manager interviewed one of the team about his experience and how his job had improved since the change and published this in the organisation's newsletter to indicate to other users and senior leaders that benefits were already being realised due to the EDRMS.

References and further reading

Blake, I. 2014. Project Management. In Smith, R., King, D., Sidhu, R. and Skelsey, D., eds. *The Effective Change Manager's Handbook*. London: Kogan Page, pp. 329–366

Cameron, E. and Green, M. 2009. *Making Sense of Change Management*. 2nd ed. London: Kogan Page

Kotter, John P. 1995. Leading Change: Why Transformation Efforts Fail. *Harvard Business Review*, [online]. Available at: <https://hbr.org/1995/05/leading-change-why-transformation-efforts-fail-2> [Accessed 12 January 2017]

Kotter, John P. 2012. *Leading Change, With New Preface by Author*. Boston: Harvard Business Review Press

Moss Kanter, R. 2009. Change Is Hardest in the Middle. *Harvard Business Review*, [online]. Available at: <https://hbr.org/2009/08/change-is-hardest-in-the-middl> [Accessed 12 January 2017]

11 Shaping sustainable change

The risk of declaring victory too soon (Kotter, 1995)

Many projects end when the change has been implemented – the product is put into service and is working to an agreed level, users have been trained on any associated activities, and an agreed period of post-implementation support has been supplied, often known as 'hypercare'. At this point, it is common to celebrate success and lose sight of the fact that the change is far from complete. A challenging time still lays ahead whilst the change is embedded and becomes sustainable as part of business as usual.

The period after implementation is a very fragile time for change. Providing users have been engaged and involved in a positive way throughout the planning and implementation, they should make an initial effort to change. However, it is very common for people to start drifting back into old behaviours and ways of working a while after implementation. This could be because it is too much effort to keep working in new ways after the initial enthusiasm has worn off or possibly because inertia exerts a very strong force and people don't even notice they are reverting to old habits. Therefore, even if your change was implemented successfully, there is a high risk that the new ways of working will not be sustained. The benefits of the change will not be fully realised and the change will have failed.

It is vital that this embedding phase is led and managed as carefully as the planning and implementation of the change. There needs to be a way to measure and report on how the change is embedding, and a senior leader still needs to be responsible for the success of the change, removing barriers to success and resourcing any necessary embedding activities. Without these, there is a significantly reduced chance that the change will embed successfully, and there is nothing more heartbreaking than working really hard to get your stakeholders to buy into and support the implementation of a change only to watch them gently and quietly reject it and revert to old ways of working a few months after all the effort of implementation has ended.

Box 11.1   The sustainability threat to Mayer & Co e-file

The e-file implementation at Mayer & Co was completed within five months. After a short productivity dip during the first couple of weeks of implementation, operational figures showed the same level of productivity as before the change. Users fed back that the engagement activities, training, and post-implementation support from the champions was very helpful. All indicators were pointing to a successful change.

Yet in the weeks following implementation, satisfaction with the new system deteriorated. Champions and team managers began receiving reports that users were finding the system difficult to work with, that reading from a screen was slowing users down, and that they were worried they would overlook vital information by not being able to flick through paper files. The scanning department began receiving requests from individual caseworkers for the original paper case files, and anecdotal evidence increased that other people were printing out their files to work from in paper.

Even though the performance figures were not showing any visible drop in performance or productivity, it was obvious to the business change manager that the change was in danger of failing to embed. If no targeted interventions were to take place, there was a high risk that more people would give up their efforts to learn and use the e-file, and the use of paper files would increase until e-file became obsolete and the change would have failed.

How long does it take to embed change?

This is really dependent on the type of change you are putting in, the culture of your organisation, how easy it is to measure and report on progress, and how committed your senior leaders are to really making a change.

It is also dependent on how often the tasks and activities which have changed are carried out. If they are done regularly, for example every day as part of a daily work routine, it will take less time for the new ways of working to be repeated enough to be embedded, perhaps only a few months. If users only have to engage in the new ways of working less regularly, for example at the end of every quarter or year, or if the change requires a more fundamental cultural change, it may take years to fully embed.

If the benefits of your change are purely quantitative, for example reducing costs or headcount, or increasing income or profit, you may be tempted to assume that the change has been embedded successfully once these benefits have been realised. From one perspective, this is true. However, other elements needed for the change to successfully embed and become business as usual may have been overlooked because they were not being measured as benefits. The example of Spark Clearholme's finance department restructure in Chapter 2 illustrates this perfectly. The restructure had been put in place with people in all the new roles, but as time went on, it was becoming clear that the department was struggling to work efficiently and happily within the new structure. If the only benefit being measured from the change was that all new roles in the target operating model were filled, and the final headcount was less than that of the two original companies, the change could be seen as being successful. However, if well-being of staff, individual workloads, and quality of output were also being measured as benefits of the change, the success of the change might be in question.

Therefore, you may need to measure a number of additional indicators as well as the official expected benefits of the change to make sure that your change is embedded successfully and really adding value to the organisation.

Box 11.2   Success measures for Mayer & Co e-file

Following the deterioration of support for the newly implemented e-file, the project sponsor and business change manager decided to put together a range of measures that would indicate when Mayer & Co's e-file could be seen as being successfully embedded. These included tangible measures to indicate that the system was being used and more intangible measures to ensure that users were happy with the system. Table 11.1 outlines these measures. Note that it does not require 100% of users to have changed to the new ways of working for the organisation to benefit from the change. There would always be a few cases which were too large or complex to work in e-file, and the project sponsor accepted that there may always be a few caseworkers who printed out their files, regardless of what they were supposed to do. Proving the vast majority used e-file, these anomalies would not adversely affect the benefits of the e-file system.

What can you do to help embed your change?

The type of activities you choose to carry out to help embed your change will be dependent on the individual circumstances you are working in. You will probably need to organise a number of activities, which together will lead to successful embedding. The following are some ideas:

- Try to make it impossible to go back to old ways of working. For example turn off old IT systems to ensure people use new ones and get rid of shelving space to help with paper reduction changes.
- Make symbolic changes to remind people to work in new ways. For example physically move people to new desks to augment a restructure or amend the dress code to enhance a cultural change.

Table 11.1 Success measures for Mayer & Co e-file

Activity	Measurement	Aim	Evidence
Caseworkers access e-file on a regular basis	Number of people logging into e-file	90% of caseworkers logging in at least three times a week	Log-in reports automatically generated by e-file system
Caseworkers accessing and working on cases through e-file	Number of requests to scanning department for paper case files	No more than 5% of all cases requested per month for six months	Manual report from the scanning department of requests
Caseworkers accessing and working on cases through e-file	Number of people printing electronic files locally	Less than 5% of caseworkers to print electronic files locally	Anecdotal evidence from e-file champions and team managers
Caseworkers working as or more efficiently with e-file than paper cases	Number of cases completed	90% of all pre e-file completion targets met or exceeded for three consecutive quarters	Automatically generated operational performance reports
Caseworkers confident in working in e-file	Number of questions and issues raised	Questions and issues reduced by 90% from first month of roll out	Manual reports from e-file champions
Caseworkers confident in working in e-file	Individual learning progress sheets (see Chapter 9)	90% of users have completed progress sheets	Team manager records of progress sheets
Caseworkers willing and/or happy to work in e-file	General temperature check	Informal comments, questions, and feedback by local teams	Manual qualitative evidence from champions and team managers
Caseworkers willing and/or happy to work in e-file	'Happiness' survey	Survey sent to all caseworkers asking how they feel about working in e-file	20% increase in satisfaction at eighteen months from baseline survey

- Continue to work with users to improve the products and associated activities implemented during the change. As people become more familiar with new ways of working, they will be able to suggest amendments which could continue to improve user experience of the change.
- Measure what is happening. For example see if you can get a report on the number of times individuals log on to a new system to ascertain adoption. Keep measuring over a period of time to check that change is embedding and people are not reverting to old ways of working.
- Make sure personal objectives, operational targets, and core competencies are amended to reflect the new behaviours and ways of working.
- Ensure any relevant organisational policies, processes, and strategies are updated to incorporate the changes.

- Ask your champions or team leaders to observe their colleagues and feedback on what people are informally saying and doing regarding the change.
- Encourage your leaders to lead by example by ensuring they and their teams visibly adopt the change.
- Keep in touch with users to gather best practice hints and tips and disseminate these to others through extra training, drop-in sessions, champion support, videos, and articles in newsletters.
- Keep the profile of the change high. Make sure key stakeholders and users are aware of quick wins, good feedback, and benefits realised.
- Set up user groups (similar to champion networks but operate in business as usual) to feedback best practice, ongoing issues, and ideas for potential improvements to the change.

Box 11.3   Embedding e-file at Mayer & Co

After developing the success criteria for e-file at Mayer & Co, the project sponsor decided that the best way to tackle the challenges of embedding was to set up another dedicated project. The Working Electronically project kept the same sponsor and project board, but a new business change project manager was appointed who had been a department head within Mayer & Co for many years and was highly respected by his colleagues, team managers, and caseworkers. He also had in-depth knowledge of casework, so was able to focus his attention very quickly on trying to improve the issues being reported by users.

He set up a series of focus groups with users to learn more about the causes of user complaints and sent out a 'happiness survey' to quantify the anecdotal feedback about people's reactions to e-file. From these, he came up with a list of things that people were finding troublesome about the new ways of working and organised them into four workstreams for the project to focus on:

1   Technical improvements to the e-file system to make it easier to use;
2   Training users in best practice to make interacting with e-file easier;
3   Developing and amending policies so they reflected how things were done with e-file, rather than paper files;
4   Communicating quick wins, early benefits realisation, and progress of the project to regain user enthusiasm and rebuild their confidence of e-file.

The project manager regularly took the success measurements to chart progress and after eighteen months resent the 'happiness survey'. At this point, all success measures were met and the change initiative could finally be handed over to business as usual.

Handing over to business as usual

There will come a time when the change team disband and the change has to become part of business as usual. This may be as soon as the implementation has been completed or after a period of post-implementation targeted support or hypercare, but it is normally a considerable time before the change is completely embedded within the organisation.

Therefore, responsibility for embedding the change may not rest with you. If this is the case, it can be difficult to relinquish control when you know that users are still uncertain about the new ways of working, the change is still very fragile, and it is by no means certain that everyone will adopt and embed the change in the way needed for the benefits to be realised. You need to ensure you can hand the change over to someone in business as usual who will continue to manage the embedding activities, run user groups, measure success, and take any remedial action needed if the change starts to falter in the coming weeks or months. The change also needs to be continued to be owned by a senior leader, who becomes responsible for the ongoing success of the change and realising the benefits.

Try to get these roles organised before your original change team disbands and ideally before implementation commences. Your senior leaders may need some convincing to continue to invest in the change once implementation is completed, as organisational pressures mean that they will be keen to move resources and attention onto the next priority. If so, adopting acceptance criteria similar to that described for the business readiness assessment in Chapter 9 may help. You could devise a set of statements which need to be signed off by representatives from all stakeholder groups to show they are happy that the change is fully embedded in business as usual before the change team can disband. Refusal to sign by trusted stakeholders may help to convince your senior leaders to continue to invest in the change until it is fully embedded.

Table 11.2 shows how some of the example change initiatives were handed over to business as usual.

Practicalities of handing over to business as usual

Handing your change initiative over to business as usual is a huge milestone and will need some proactive management for it to be successful. Following are some tips to help you manage the transition smoothly:

- Spend some time with the new manager of the change to make sure they have the complete history of the change to this point, including all your original analysis on culture, impact, and stakeholders; a comprehensive briefing about how your key stakeholders have acted during the change and where they sit now in terms of support and enthusiasm; and where you see the biggest challenges and opportunities during embedding. Introduce them to the people who will be key in embedding the change, including champions and project colleagues and any supportive senior leaders.

Table 11.2 Handing example change initiatives to business as usual

Change	Business as Usual Manager	Business as Usual Leader	User Group	Handover Details
Burntwood's EDRMS	A new post of EDRMS business benefits manager was created for three years after implementation.	The deputy CEO took responsibility for the leadership and ultimate success of the EDRMS.	An EDRMS expert community was created from the original group of champions. The group met quarterly with the business benefits manager to share best practice and local issues and to suggest improvements.	Four weeks after implementation, every team manager met with the business change manager and local champion to go through a list of sign off criteria. If these were met, the team moved over to business as usual. If not, the team remained under the care of the change project until the criteria were met.
Workout!'s Restructure	A new ongoing post of operations manager was created to manage the employment service areas (ESAs).	Head of Education Services managed the operations manager and took overall responsibility for the ESAs.	All new ESA assistants reported into the operations manager.	Once each ESA area had been implemented and the ESA assistant was in post and inducted, the area moved under the operations manager.
Mayer & Co's E-file	A new project to embed e-file was set up led by a full-time business change project manager, with the expectation of it running for at least eighteen months.	The project sponsor remained the same.	The e-file champion group remained the same	E-file moved under the management of the embedding project three months after implementation completed.
Spark Clearholme's Office Move	The facilities manager, who used to manage the old offices, became responsible for managing the new offices.	Head of Facilities continued to hold responsibility for all office space.	The relocation group met quarterly to discuss ongoing issues and ideas about the new offices.	Handover took place as soon as everyone had moved into the new offices and the relocation group were not reporting any issues. This was about three weeks after implementation completed.

- Disband the champion network if it is not continuing into business as usual. Hold an event to thank the champions for all their hard work and to celebrate the success of implementation. Try to arrange for the champions to be acknowledged by the senior leaders of your change, for example by asking the change sponsor to give a speech at the thank you event or asking them to sign individual thank you cards for each of the champions.
- Issue very clear communications to all stakeholders about the closure of the change project, what is happening next, and where they should now go for support. Put reminders on any telephone or email addresses which are being disbanded with the change project and which users or other stakeholders have been using to contact you.
- Hold debriefing sessions with champions, change colleagues, and key stake-holders to analyse the successes of the change approach and to record what could have been done better. Often called 'lessons learned', this is a very important activity to complete. Not only does it create useful information for any future change projects, but also it gives you and your colleagues an opportunity to reflect on your successes. It can also be cathartic to discuss any failures, areas of stress, or frustrations where things could have gone better.
- If you are moving on from the organisation, make sure all champions and other colleagues have your contact details in case they need to ask you for a reference regarding the work they did with you. It is surprising how many champions use their change experiences to quickly develop their careers and move into new roles.
- If you are staying in the organisation but moving onto new work, make sure you let everyone relevant know that you are no longer working on this change but that you may be contacting them shortly to discuss your next challenge!
- Thank all your senior leaders, key decision makers, middle managers, and anyone else from the organisation who has assisted you in preparing and implementing the change. They may have done the work as part of their business as usual roles but recognising and appreciating all contributions can do no harm and may leave people in a stronger and more confident frame of mind for their next change challenge.

And, finally, make sure you give yourself some time to recover and reflect before you move onto your next change. You need to greet your next group of stake-holders with as much energy, focus, and enthusiasm as you did your last in order to support them through their challenges and make their experience of change as positive as you can.

References and further reading

Bridges, W. 2009. *Managing Transitions: Making the Most of Change*. 3rd ed. London: Nicholas Brearly

Cameron, E. and Green, M. 2009. *Making Sense of Change Management*. 2nd ed. London: Kogan Page

Campbell, H. 2014. Sustaining Change. In Smith, R., King, D., Sidhu, R. and Skelsey, D., eds. *The Effective Change Manager's Handbook*. London: Kogan Page, pp. 454–491

Kotter, John P. 1995. Leading Change: Why Transformation Efforts Fail. *Harvard Business Review*, [online]. Available at: <https://hbr.org/1995/05/leading-change-why-transformation-efforts-fail-2> [Accessed 12 January 2017]

Kotter, John P. 2012. *Leading Change, With New Preface by Author*. Boston: Harvard Business Review Press

Kotter, John P. and Cohen, Dan S. 2002. *The Heart of Change*. Boston: Harvard Business Review Press

Appendix A

Example change initiatives

Burntwood EDRMS

Burntwood County Council is situated in the North East of England. It is responsible for providing a wide variety of services to the county of Burntwood, including education, social services for children and adults, highways, libraries, waste disposal, and town and country planning. Burntwood employs around 2,000 staff. Its main sources of income are government grants, council tax, and redistributed business rates.

The EDRMS programme aims to improve electronic information management across Burntwood. An EDRMS is an Electronic Document Records Management System, a type of content management system which allows organisations to manage electronic documents and records throughout the document life cycle.

Mayer & Co e-file

Mayer & Co is a law firm based in Bristol. They have 300 solicitors and 1,000 paralegal caseworkers dealing with 2,000 new cases and working on approximately 7,000 cases each year. There are three departments dealing with Family Law, Employment Law, and Property Law. Caseworkers deal with correspondence, prepare legal cases, and attend to client queries.

Currently, all correspondence and legal cases are paper based. The e-file project aims to convert these to electronic cases by scanning all postal correspondence and creating and saving documents to e-file rather than printing out and adding to the paper files.

Workout! restructure

Workout! is a UK-wide employment charity whose aim is to help job seekers into employment. It has 150 volunteer-run branches throughout the UK who organise and run employment courses with paid instructors and additional support activities by volunteers. The branches are supported by a small London-based office of paid employees, led by the Chief Executive Officer (CEO), who set strategy, undertake research and fundraising, and support the branches with infrastructure functions such as finance, HR, and technology.

Workout! is undergoing a major restructure of how it runs its courses by amalgamating branches to form sixty larger employment service areas (ESAs). Each of these will employ a paid ESA assistant who will arrange and book courses for the area. A new booking and finance system to be used across all areas and linking into the central office will also be implemented.

Spark Clearholme merger

Sparks and Clearholme are two electrical goods companies based in the Midlands who have recently merged to form Spark Clearholme – the largest electrical goods retailer in Europe. Shortly before the merger, a project management office was set up to develop and run the 200 change initiatives needed to consolidate the new company. Four of these change initiatives are as follows:

Office move

Sparks and Clearholme each had two offices before the merger. Spark Clearholme has been operating out of these old offices since the merger took place. They are now going to move the new company into one purpose-built office block in a business park near to the location of the old offices.

Marketing campaign planner

Spark Clearholme has a central marketing team who supports ten different departments with planning and running the marketing campaigns for their electrical goods. Hundreds of marketing campaigns are run each year. The marketing campaign planner is a piece of software in which all marketing information can be entered in order to compare activities and costs of each campaign. The marketing team are hoping this will provide useful business intelligence reports showing which campaigns are most successful and why.

Finance department restructure

Spark Clearholme's finance department has been created from the finance teams of the two original companies. During the early days of the merger, the department continued to operate as two separate teams whilst the head of finance developed a target operating model for the new department. The restructure consists of implementing the new operating model and accompanying it with cultural and behavioural changes to form one united finance department for Spark Clearholme.

Appendix B

Change plan for the Burntwood EDRMS programme

Change initiative 1: engaging leaders and making the case for change

Issue: Major risk of resistance to new ways of working from all levels of the organisation.

Activity: Face-to-face meetings with all senior leaders across organisation (approximately sixty):

- Inform them of aims of programme;
- Make the case for change by emphasising the drivers for change;
- Find out questions, issues, and suggested improvements from leaders based on the knowledge of their teams and culture of the organisation;
- Outline next steps and gain their commitment to actively supporting the programme.

Desired outcome: Increased buy-in and decreased resistance from the top of the organisation.

Measurement: After meeting, senior leaders feel positive about the change and actively lead their teams through the transition, giving staff time to engage with the programme and encouraging them through the challenges of transition.

Change initiative 2: involving users at a local level – creating a change champion network

Issue: Changes to behaviour and culture need to happen at a very local level within the organisation, involving 150 teams and 1,800 individuals.

Activity: Set up EDRMS champion network – sixty users based in the business who can communicate programme messages to their colleagues and feedback issues, suggestions, and problems to the programme.

Desired outcome: Local intelligence gathered from the champions will enable the programme to tailor support and interventions depending on the impact of the change on teams, the level of enthusiasm or resistance to the change, and the influential capacity of individuals within the team.

Measurement: Champions in each local area gathering feedback and teams engaged and bought into the change through tailored support and intervention from individual champions.

Change initiative 3: small steps and quick wins

Issue: Affected users need to accept significant changes to their ways of working and maintain interest in the programme through a long procurement and development process where users will see very little immediate change.

Activity: Build in some small changes and quick wins before the implementation of the EDRMS by visiting each team with a menu of suggested small changes they can make to their information management behaviours which would result in a small improvement for the team.

Desired outcome: Users find quick benefits through adopting just one small change, for example being able to find key documents more quickly because they were named properly.

Measurement: Increased interest in information management and individuals and teams have increased confidence to explore the bigger changes brought by the implementation of the EDRMS.

Change initiative 4: user involvement in EDRMS development

Issue: Greater chance of resistance if EDRMS is imposed on users and they have no involvement in designing the new product or associated activities.

Activity: Prior to implementation, set up a model office where champions and other key stakeholders can try out the EDRMS in a safe environment and feedback how it would work with their current activities and processes.

Desired outcome: Each local area decides on the best ways of using the EDRMS to accommodate their working practices and, where relevant, modify their processes to get more benefits from the EDRMS.

Measurement: Each local area is confident that their local activities and processes will work with the system, having modified them if necessary.

Change initiative 5: learning and training

Issue: Implementing the EDRMS means a big change in the way users manage their information. There are also risks involved with the misuse of the EDRMS, for example sophisticated access controls mean that users must store their information in the correct folders to prevent confidential information being distributed inappropriately.

Activity: A two-hour classroom-based training session to be developed and to be mandatory for all users – including the CEO and executive team. After the training, users to be given fact sheets and video clips covering all aspects of the system to refer to as they get used to using the system. Floorwalking is to be provided for four weeks after implementation to check for technological and user issues and support users during the early days of the change.

Desired outcome: Users use the EDRMS properly.

Measurement: Amount and types of questions for floorwalkers after implementation. Correct usage of the system.

Change initiative 6: communicating good news stories and early benefits realisation

Issue: Implementation is phased, meaning what happens to early teams will influence the buy-in of later teams. Senior managers need to support the change despite disruption to business as usual during implementation and embedding.

Activity: At the end of the implementation of each team, hold a meeting with each team leader and champion to sign off the implementation. At this point, identify good news stories and early benefits and communicate these out to the organisation, especially to teams still to be implemented to allay fears and increase buy-in.

Desired outcome: Teams still to implement increase their buy-in and enthusiasm due to good news stories. Some supportive senior managers to be implemented early in the roll out and their good news stories to add gravitas to the implementation and overcome resistance in other parts of the organisation.

Measurement: Teams still to roll out have increased buy-in and enthusiasm for the programme. Increased general enthusiasm for the programme and increased awareness of the benefits of the change.

Change initiative 7: making the change stick once the roll out has been completed

Issue: Embedding the necessary changes in behaviour and culture will take much longer than the length of the programme set up to deliver the change.

Activity: At the end of the programme, hand ownership of EDRMS to the business to carry out this work, including a new full-time role of business benefits manager and setting up local EDRMS user groups in departments, owned and run by enthusiastic employees.

Desired outcome: EDRMS, behaviours, and cultures will continue to embed and increased benefits will continue to be realised over the months and years after the implementation.

Measurement: Increased benefits, good news stories, new ways of working enabled by EDRMS.

Index